Spark

KEEPER OF THE FLAME FOR EMERGING LEADERS

SPARK: Keeper of the Flame for Emerging Leaders
A Companion for Parents, Mentors, and Guardians

Published by:
Executive Books | Tremendous Life Books
P.O. Box 267, Boiling Springs, PA 17007
717-701-8159 | 800-233-2665
www.TremendousLeadership.com

Paperback ISBN: 978-1-961202-56-6
Ebook ISBN: 978-1-961202-57-3

Spark

KEEPER OF THE FLAME FOR EMERGING LEADERS

A COMPANION FOR PARENTS, MENTORS, AND GUARDIANS

DR. TRACEY C. JONES

TABLE OF CONTENTS

DEDICATION TO THE GENERATIONS

I am writing to you, fathers, because you know him who is from the beginning. I am writing to you, young men, because you have overcome the evil one.

I write to you, dear children, because you know the Father. I write to you, fathers, because you know him who is from the beginning.

I write to you, young men, because you are strong, and the word of God lives in you, and you have overcome the evil one.

(1 John 2:13–14)

To the parents:
Because you know Him who is from the beginning.
Because you have walked through seasons and storms—and still call Him faithful.

To the teens and emerging leaders:
Because you are strong.
Because the Word of God abides in you.
Because you have overcome the evil one.

To all of us—young and old:
Because we are forgiven.
Because we know the Father.
Because we walk together in truth.

This book is for you. All of you. Because God's plan was always generational.

BEFORE WE BEGIN

Throughout this book, I use the word "parent" to describe more than just biological mothers and fathers. It includes mentors, teachers, coaches, neighbors, siblings, pastors, and anyone who invests in the life of a young person. You may not have children of your own, but if you are pouring truth, time, and love into an emerging leader, you are fulfilling a sacred parental role.

I don't have biological children myself, but I've had the joy and responsibility of serving as a spiritual auntie to countless young people. I've mentored, taught, led, coached, and prayed over the next generation—and I consider it one of the greatest privileges of my life. If that's you too, welcome. This book is yours as much as it is theirs.

And for those of you who followed God's first commandment to "be fruitful and multiply"—bless your socks off for bringing children into this world! You have welcomed both joy and responsibility into your life, and I pray this book blesses you as you raise, guide, and launch the legacy God has entrusted to you.

FOREWORD

Called From the Start

God doesn't wait for adulthood to call His chosen. Many of the greatest leaders and prophets were set apart as children—even before birth. Scripture is full of divine callings that begin not in maturity, but in infancy or the womb itself. Isaac was promised before conception as the child of covenant (Genesis 17:19). Moses was born during a genocide, yet preserved and raised in Pharaoh's court to deliver a nation (Exodus 2). Samuel heard God's voice while still a child serving in the temple (1 Samuel 3). David, the youngest of eight brothers, was anointed king while still tending sheep (1 Samuel 16). Jeremiah was told, *"Before I formed you in the womb I knew you"* (Jeremiah 1:5). John the Baptist leapt in the womb when Jesus approached (Luke 1:41), and Jesus Himself, our Savior, was both fully divine and fully human from conception. These aren't just stories of youth—they are holy reminders that God begins His work early.

I didn't have prophetic dreams or leap in the womb like some of God's mighty prophets. But I remember, even as a young teen, longing to know God's purpose for my life. One day, my father looked at me and said, "There's something special about you." That simple statement confirmed what I already hoped was true: I was set apart. Not just another teenager, but a vessel God could use. I share that memory to encourage you—if you see something sacred in your child, say it. Your words can water what God has already planted.

But these children didn't rise in isolation. Behind every chosen child was a parent or guardian who saw the spark of destiny and responded in faith. Abraham trusted God to raise Isaac. Jochebed placed baby Moses in the Nile, believing in divine protection. Hannah surrendered her long-awaited son Samuel to temple life. Jesse sent young David to Saul's court, then to battle. Zechariah and Elizabeth nurtured John in righteousness, while Mary and Joseph, misunderstood and maligned, guarded Jesus' early life with fierce obedience. These parents didn't always understand the full picture, but they recognized God's hand—and they trusted Him more than their own plans.

As you walk alongside your own emerging leader, remember: their SPARK is not random—it is revealed. SPARK is not about being molded into someone else's image, but unfolded into the design God has already placed within them. And just as He guided those ancient parents, He will guide you too.

INTRODUCTION

CONGRATULATIONS! You have raised a child who aspires to become the greatest version of themselves. This doesn't happen without your diligence and intentionality. Your focus and sacrifice in raising them to this point in life will pay incredible dividends in their future. They may not know it yet, but rest assured, you did TREMENDOUS!

Society will thank you for unleashing a functioning, adjusted, industrious, and ethical member into its workforce. You glorify God by the discipleship you imparted. That is why He entrusted this child into your care.

> **"Our very survival depends on the effective social commitments of hardworking, caring, and emotionally stable adults who need to step up to the plate, in the prime of their lives, and take on the most daunting adaptive challenges that face the group."**
>
> Dr. Dan P. McAdams, *The Art and Science of Personality Development*

But now, it's time for them to begin their departure from your guardianship as they navigate their space and place in the world and define their sense of self. Did you know there's actual science behind this transition?

During adolescence, the brain undergoes significant hormonal and structural changes that influence behavior and identity formation. Oxytocin, often called the "hug hormone," for its role in social bonding, experiences fluctuations during this period. Research suggests that alterations in oxytocin levels may contribute to the social and emotional shifts observed in teenagers, such as decreased affiliative behaviors and an increased focus on independence.

This natural transition allows adolescents to step back from familial attachments and explore their own identities, fostering autonomy, and helping them form a unique sense of self. Understanding these changes can help parents provide support and encouragement as their teens navigate this critical stage of development. In other words, it's not you....it's them. They don't want to hug and talk like they used to, and that's scientific, and it's also scriptural!

We can see this play out in the Bible in Luke 2:49–52, where Jesus got separated from his parents when they traveled to Jerusalem for the feast of the Passover. When the emerging leader, our teen Lord, was found teaching in the synagogue (three days later!), Mary was upset, hurt, and unimpressed with her teen's inspired words to the leaders, exclaiming, "Young man, why have you done this to us? Your father and I have been half out of our minds looking for you."

Jesus' response perfectly illustrates this transition time: "Why were you looking for me? Didn't you know that I had to be here, dealing with the things of My Father?" As Jesus began stepping into His calling as a teen, we see something I learned in my doctoral classes regarding childhood development. Psychologist Paul Baltes proposed the term "Arc of Maturation."

Adolescence is a period of maturation that involves a range of physiological, cognitive, and emotional changes. This period is marked by both growth and decline in various domains, reflecting the dynamic nature of development. Understanding this nuanced progression can help parents support their teens through the multifaceted journey of adolescence, ensuring respect for the hierarchy of parent and child, while encouraging the development of the teen's sense of self.

Your Hopes, Their Future

As a parent or guardian, you hold a vision for your child that is as unique as they are. From their earliest days, you've nurtured their dreams, celebrated their milestones, and quietly hoped they would find a life filled with purpose and joy. You've imagined a future where they confidently step into their potential, navigating life with courage, wisdom, and grace.

But the journey to greatness isn't always straightforward—especially in today's complex world. Social pressures, self-doubt, and the sheer volume of choices young people face can make it challenging for them to see the potential that's so clear to you. Growing up as a teen in today's world is different in some respects from what we experienced, but rest assured, the challenges and temptations thrown at them by the prince of the power of the air (Ephesians 2:2) are as old as time.

Yet, as believers, we know that this vision isn't just ours. It's rooted in God's design for your child. The Bible reminds us: *"For we are God's handiwork, created in Christ Jesus to do good works, which God prepared in advance for us to do"* (Ephesians 2:10). Your child's life has been crafted with divine purpose, and you are entrusted with the sacred responsibility of guiding them toward that purpose.

How do you help your teen navigate this season of life? How can you support them in discovering their passions, embracing their strengths, and developing the skills they'll need to thrive? These questions are at the heart of this book, and the SPARK construct is a simple and straightforward resource that you can apply and modify.

Lighting the Way for the Next Generation

I penned *SPARK: The Five Essentials to Ignite the Greatness Within* in 2020. The book was the result of my doctoral research on self-efficacy, a Ph.D. word for motivation and confidence. My research revealed that greatness is already in each of us; we just have to work to unfold it. My sole purpose in life is to help others see the *Image Dei*—the Latin term meaning "Image of God"— inside themselves that God has breathed in (Genesis 2:7). The working out of this divine nature autograph (DNA) is on us.

When Arthur Woods, my co-author, approached me about translating the five essentials into a version for emerging and aspiring teen leaders, my self-efficacy popped! I was a product of parents, teachers, pastors, guardians, influencers, and leaders who poured into me with books, correction, encouragement, rebuke, and counsel. Arthur is a renowned speaker, teacher, and now author, to this tremendous demographic of individuals....teens, or as we often refer to them in this book, emerging leaders.

Even as a fiercely independent teenager, I knew the adults I admired had already figured life out because they were where I wanted to go. I watched and I listened. I traveled with my father on countless trips from the time I was four years old. These men and women modeled grace, integrity, faith, service, generosity, appearance, and health. I followed, fascinated, slowly but surely; I knew they had my best interests at heart regardless of my eye rolls, lack of gratitude, snark, procrastination, and indifference. This is who I wanted to become; and I knew even as a youngster that this goal was up to me.

This book invites you to model, encourage, and equip your teen with the tools they need to discover and ignite the greatness God has placed within them, and to allow God to use them to teach you in the process. And in the process, I know you'll be blessed too because truth is timeless. What works for adults are the same foundational principles that work for teens.

"God never gave my kids to me for me to teach them. He gave me to them for them to teach me."

Charlie "Tremendous" Jones, *The Key to Excellence*

SPARK is more than a leadership model. It's a discipleship framework, a development guide, and a practical and spiritual invitation to grow alongside your teen while helping them become everything God created them to be. It's ageless, and timeless, because it is rooted in God's truths about calling and equipping.

Let's get started and build a fortress for families, one holy SPARK at a time.

The Trevor Parallel: A Parent's Perspective

In *SPARK for Emerging Leaders*, Arthur opens with a story about Trevor, a teenager who feels stuck in the middle of the pack—not exceptional, not failing—just ordinary. As Trevor scrolls through social media, he compares his life to others, and concludes that he doesn't have anything worth celebrating. He isn't bitter, but he is discouraged. Despite being surrounded by people, he feels overlooked and underwhelmed by his own potential.

That is, until an unexpected school assembly introduces him to Jason, a leadership coach who challenges everything Trevor believes about himself. Jason tells the students that greatness isn't reserved for the gifted or the bold—it's available to anyone willing to lean into growth. Though skeptical, Trevor is intrigued. When Jason hands him a copy of *SPARK*, something shifts. For the first time in a long time, Trevor feels something stirring—a hope that maybe, just maybe, his story is just beginning.

Ask your teen to describe what stood out to them about Trevor's experience. Did they resonate with any of his thoughts or emotions? Have they ever felt that same "ordinary ache?"

As a parent, you may already see the seeds of greatness in your teen—gifts, glimmers, and godly potential waiting to bloom. But in seasons of uncertainty, when hormones flare, and confidence falters, they may not be able to see it for themselves. That's when they'll need to borrow your belief. Of course, there may also be moments when you wonder if greatness is even remotely in the picture—when your child's choices, attitudes, or behaviors feel more like those of a tiny demon than a budding disciple (Your spouse might even joke that this book should've been titled *SPANK* instead of *SPARK!*).

Take heart. These moments don't define your child or their future. They're simply part of the journey—an invitation to grow in grace, for both of you. Stay the course and cling to God's promise: *"For I know the plans I have for you," declares the Lord, "plans to prosper you and not to harm you, plans to give you hope and a future"* (Jeremiah 29:11).

Trevor's story reminds us that greatness often begins with a faint but real whisper of hope. With the right tools, guidance, and voices in their lives, our teens can rise to meet the future God has prepared for them. Like Jason did for Trevor, you serve as a pivotal voice in your child's life.

You are their first and most enduring rabbi—their teacher of teachers.

Your role matters deeply, especially in a culture bent on distracting, distorting, and deceiving the hearts and minds of young people. But take courage: *"For everyone born of God overcomes the world. This is the victory that has overcome the world, even our faith"* (1 John 5:4).

As you read this companion guide alongside your teen, may you both be equipped and encouraged. You'll not only nurture their confidence, character, and calling—you'll also find yourself being transformed. Parenting is one of God's most profound training programs. During an interview, Charlie "Tremendous" Jones had this to say when asked about the best training programs for leaders (https://www.leadernetwork.org/charlie_jones_february_06.htm):

> *"For me, though, the greatest training program in my life was not the courses I took at Purdue or LSU or any of the schools: My greatest training program was teaching Sunday school with eight-year-olds. It disciplined me to study each week to teach these young people the Bible. I never taught that much, but I sure learned a lot. I have seen great results and success in many young men's lives because they took my counsel and taught Sunday School."*

Welcome to the SPARK journey. Your child's story—and yours—is just beginning.

What You'll Discover

SPARK for Emerging Leaders and *Keeper of the Flame* is more than a framework; it's a way to inspire and empower your teen to dream bigger and achieve more. But it's also designed with you in mind—because no one impacts a child's growth more than thc adults who love and support them.

The SPARK Framework is built on five essential elements that help emerging leaders move from potential to purpose. As a parent, mentor, or guardian, your role is to walk alongside your teen as they grow in confidence and character.

The first two components—Singularity and Persistence—are primarily *internal.* These are matters of identity and personal grit. Your child must discover their God-given purpose and develop the perseverance to pursue it. Your job is to model these qualities, speak them over your teen, and help them recognize how God shapes their inner world. Only God knows the calling He has placed on your teen's life. And only your teen can do the personal work required to step into it. But your influence in helping cultivate these internal qualities is immeasurable.

The final three components—Advocates, Resources, and Knowledge—are primarily *external.* These represent the people, tools, opportunities, and information your teen will need to fulfill their calling. As a parent, your goal is to help them recognize who and what is already around them, identify what they still need, and guide them toward the support structures that will launch them forward. You also need to be the strict gatekeeper about what is allowed into their lives. Their brains aren't fully developed to critically reason and think about future consequences, so it's up to you to guard them at all costs.

Here's what we'll explore together and a brief description of the five essentials that comprise S.P.A.R.K.:

1. **Singularity:** Helping your child discover their unique passions, strengths, and purpose while honoring the individuality that sets them apart. Singularity is about recognizing that God has made your child with a unique design and calling. While the world may try to push them toward conformity or comparison, your role is to help them focus on their God-given identity. This support means helping them uncover their gifts, talents, and interests and affirming that they are *fearfully and wonderfully made* (Psalm 139:14).

   Encourage your teen to seek clarity in their purpose, guiding them to reflect on what truly excites them or brings them joy. Singularity isn't about perfection or instant clarity—it's about the journey of learning who God created them to be and stepping into that truth with confidence. Together, you can explore their passions, test their strengths, and celebrate the individuality that sets them apart for God's glory.

2. **Persistence:** Teaching resilience and grit—showing them how to embrace challenges, learn from failures, and keep moving forward. Life will throw obstacles in your child's path, and how they respond will define their journey. Persistence is about equipping them to see challenges as opportunities to grow. Remind them of the biblical truth that *"Not only so, but we also glory in our sufferings, because we know that suffering produces perseverance; perseverance, character; and character, hope"* (Romans 5:3–4). Failure isn't the end—it's part of God's refining process.

   As a parent, model persistence by showing them how you tackle setbacks with faith and determination. Share stories of your own challenges and how God brought you through. Teach them to pray through difficulty, to lean on God's strength, and to trust His timing. With your encouragement, they'll learn that resilience isn't just about getting back up—it's about trusting that God is working in all things for their good (Romans 8:28).

3. **Advocates:** Building a network of mentors, role models, and supporters who can encourage and guide them. Your teen was never meant to navigate life alone, and neither were you. Advocates are people who come alongside them to offer wisdom, encouragement, and guidance. This person could be a teacher, a coach, a youth pastor, or even a trusted family member. Proverbs 15:22 reminds us: *"Plans fail for lack of counsel, but with many advisers they succeed."*

Help your teen identify and connect with godly advocates who can walk with them through life's challenges. Encourage them to seek relationships with those who reflect Christ-like character and who will inspire and challenge them to grow. At the same time, remember that you are one of their most important advocates. Your love, prayers, and presence speak volumes, reminding them daily that they are supported and deeply valued.

4. **Resources:** Identifying and leveraging the tools, experiences, and opportunities that can fuel their growth. Resources are the practical pieces of the puzzle that help your teen move forward—books, classes, programs, workshops, and even experiences like mission trips or internships. These tools provide the fuel for their development. Remind them that God equips those He calls: *"His divine power has given us everything we need for a godly life through our knowledge of Him who called us by His own glory and goodness"* (2 Peter 1:3).

   Teach your teen to be proactive in seeking out and using resources wisely. Encourage them to invest in opportunities that align with their values and goals, and model this behavior by sharing resources you've found helpful in your growth. Show them that God often places the tools right in front of us—we need to recognize and use them.

5. **Knowledge:** Instilling a love of lifelong learning and helping them use knowledge to shape their future. Knowledge is the foundation that supports your child's growth. Encourage them to approach learning not just as a way to achieve worldly success, but as a way to deepen their understanding of God's creation and their

role within it. Proverbs 1:7 says, "*The fear of the LORD is the beginning of knowledge, but fools despise wisdom and instruction.*" Help them see learning as an act of worship and a way to glorify God with their minds. Foster curiosity by discussing big ideas, exploring Scripture, and encouraging questions. Remind them that wisdom goes beyond academics—it's about applying knowledge in ways that honor God and serve others. As they grow in knowledge, they'll be better equipped to make decisions, solve problems, and fulfill their purpose.

Through these principles, you'll learn how to nurture not only their leadership potential but also their confidence, character, and sense of purpose.

Your Role as the Keeper of the Flame

Your teen's journey is uniquely theirs, but your role in that journey is irreplaceable. You vacillate between coach, cop, consultant, and caregiver. You are the steady presence that encourages them to take risks, the voice that reminds them of their worth, and the guide who helps them see opportunities they might otherwise overlook.

The Bible calls us to train our children in the way they should go: "*Train up a child in the way he should go; even when he is old he will not depart from it, even in old age*" (Proverbs 22:6, NCV). This book is your companion in this incredible role, equipping you to light the SPARK of God-given greatness in your child.

> **"So, I finally figured out the only way I can help my own kids more is learning how to hinder them less."**
>
> Charlie "Tremendous" Jones, *The Key to Excellence*

Reflection Questions

As we begin, take a moment to reflect on your hopes and goals as a parent or guardian. Use these questions to guide your thoughts and set the tone for this journey:

1. What does God's vision for your teen look like to you? How do you see His hand shaping their life?
2. How do you currently encourage your teen's spiritual, emotional, and personal growth?
3. What challenges do you face in balancing guidance with letting your teen make their own decisions?
4. What are the unique gifts, talents, and qualities God has given your teen?
5. How can you create an environment that nurtures their faith and confidence in God's plan for them?
6. How do you rely on God for wisdom and patience in your parenting journey?
7. What would success look like for your relationship with your teen as they grow into the person God has called them to be?

Parenting or mentoring a young leader is both a privilege and a challenge. But together, we'll explore how to ignite the spark of greatness in your child and glorify God through their journey. Let's begin.

SPARK

ONE

SINGULARITY: HELPING YOUR TEEN CONCENTRATE ON WHAT MATTERS

Haley's Story: A Lesson in Focus

In *SPARK for Emerging Leaders*, Arthur shares the story of Haley, a high-achieving young woman whose life is packed with potential, promise, and pressure. Ask your teen to walk you through what stood out in Haley's journey, and listen closely to what they saw and felt.

Haley was the kind of teen every parent dreams of: smart, organized, driven, and deeply involved in school, church, and community. By her early twenties, she juggled full-time college coursework, leading her sorority, interning at a prestigious marketing firm, mentoring younger students, and running a side business designing custom planners. She had a color-coded calendar and a mile-long to-do list—and she thrived on the thrill of getting things done.

Until she didn't.

Gradually, the signs of burnout crept in. Her academic performance slipped. Relationships grew distant. Her once-beloved planner business became just another item to manage. She stopped going to church and began snapping at friends. Sleep eluded her. Guilt, anxiety, and exhaustion replaced the joy she once found in excellence.

It wasn't until a chance coffee shop encounter with her old high school mentor, Veronica, that Haley had space to reflect. Veronica asked a disarming question: "*What do you want most in life?*" Haley's usual confidence faltered. The answer didn't come quickly, because for all her accomplishments, she had never stopped to clarify what they were for.

Veronica gently challenged her to define success on her own terms—not by what the world expected, but by what God had uniquely designed her to pursue. That conversation became a turning point. Haley began saying "no" to good things that weren't the *right* things. She stepped down from leadership roles, scaled back her internship hours, and poured her energy into helping others live simpler, more meaningful lives through her planner business. As her commitments narrowed, her clarity deepened. Her grades improved. Her relationships began to heal. She felt like herself again.

Invite your teen to reflect on how Haley's drive mirrors their own. Are they operating with focus—or just with fuel? Are they running toward something meaningful—or simply running?

This scenario is what your Type A teen has in store for young adulthood. You don't need to launch these high-capacity beacons—they launch themselves. But you *do* need to help them focus. They're all thrust and no vector. Think of it like a child's kaleidoscope—bursting with color but lacking alignment. Your job is to help them channel that brilliance into a white-hot laser beam of clarity-driven purpose.

Even the most disciplined, godly young people lose their way at times. It's part of growing up and, frankly, part of adulthood. But that's why your role is so critical. You are the mentor in the coffee shop. You are Veronica. You are the one who asks the questions that cut through the noise.

Don't be discouraged when your teen doesn't know the answer right away. That's not a sign of failure—it's the beginning of focus.

As the Bible says: "*Let your eyes look straight ahead; fix your gaze directly before you. Give careful thought to the paths for your feet and be steadfast in all your ways*" (Proverbs 4:25–26).

In a world that tells our teens they need to do everything, your steady guidance reminds them that it's okay—even essential—to do fewer things *well.* As you walk through this chapter together, help your child to name what matters most. Help them discover that when they embrace their God-given singularity, they'll find clarity, confidence, and peace.

Helping Your Teen Focus

Haley's story reminds us even the most talented and driven young people can struggle when their focus is scattered. In today's world, where teens face countless opportunities, distractions, and pressures, they may feel compelled to say "yes" to everything. As a parent, your role is to help them discern what truly matters and guide them toward their singular focus.

Ask your teen reflective questions like Veronica did for Haley: "What do you want most in life?" and "What does success mean to you?" These questions may not have immediate answers, but they can spark the kind of introspection that leads to clarity over time.

There is a tremendous amount of attention on Emotional Intelligence (EQ), and rightly so. Leadership scholars suggest that 85% of a person's success comes from these softer skills. The number one trait of high EQ people is self-awareness. Self-awareness is one of the most difficult yet rewarding things we do. Thanks to our Creator we do not have to do this alone. Look to King David's glorious psalm:

You have searched me, Lord,
and you know me.
2 *You know when I sit and when I rise;*
you perceive my thoughts from afar.

3 You discern my going out and my lying down;
you are familiar with all my ways.
4 Before a word is on my tongue
you, Lord, know it completely.
5 You hem me in behind and before,
and you lay your hand upon me.
6 Such knowledge is too wonderful for me,
too lofty for me to attain.
(Psalms 139:1–6)

Without guidance, teens may struggle to focus, becoming overwhelmed by the sheer number of choices they face. This challenge is where you can step in—not to dictate their path, but to help them filter out distractions and align their actions with their God-given potential.

The Power of Singularity

Haley's story reminds us that life isn't about doing more—it's about doing what matters most. As a parent, you have the privilege of helping your teen discover their North Star, the singular focus that will guide them through life's challenges and opportunities. By offering support, asking the right questions, and modeling focus in your life, you can help your teen live with clarity, purpose, and passion.

"The skill of an artist may lie in what he or she leaves out. An amateur crowds everything in."

Henrietta Meers, *What the Bible is All About*

Your Role as a Guide

The teen years are a unique and pivotal time in a young person's development. Research shows that during adolescence young people often have a clearer sense of what they'd like to do with their lives than they may later on. Their dreams are vivid, their creativity is at its peak, and they are actively shaping their identity. This is a critical window for parents to help their teens explore and refine their interests, values, and purpose.

Singularity is about helping your teen discover their unique passions, strengths, and purpose—the things that align with who they are and who God created them to be. Not every teen will follow a traditional path, and that's okay. Some may feel called to trade school, entrepreneurship, creative arts, or a less conventional route. As a parent, your job isn't to impose your own vision but to guide them toward uncovering their God-given potential.

Values: The Compass for Life

One of the best ways to help your teen discover their singular focus is to guide them in identifying their core values. Values are the principles that shape who they are and what they prioritize. When teens understand what they stand for, they gain clarity in their decisions and direction. These are foundational to everything that's to come in life.

Encourage conversations about values by asking open-ended questions like, "What do you think is most important in life?" or "Who do you admire, and why?" These discussions will help your teen begin to articulate what matters most to them. Share your own values as well—how they've guided your decisions and shaped your life. And remind them of the ultimate foundation for their values: *"The fear of the LORD is the beginning of wisdom, and knowledge of the Holy One is understanding"* (Proverbs 9:10).

Passions: Sparking Excitement

Passions are often the first clues to a teen's singular focus. What excites them? What activities make them lose track of time? Whether it's coding, building things, advocating for causes, or expressing themselves creatively, their passions are significant indicators of where their energy and talent lie.

As a parent, you can nurture these passions by providing opportunities for exploration. Take them to workshops, help them connect with mentors in their areas of interest, or encourage them to spend time doing what they love. Pay attention to what lights them up—you might even notice their excitement before they do!

Purpose: The Bigger Picture

Your teen's purpose is their "why"—the larger reason behind what they want to do. While purpose can feel daunting to define, it often emerges when values and passions intersect. As their parent, you can help them connect their talents and interests to a greater mission.

Ephesians 2:10 beautifully reminds us: *"For we are God's handiwork, created in Christ Jesus to do good works, which God prepared in advance for us to do."* Help your teen understand that their purpose is not just about personal achievement but also about serving others and glorifying God through their gifts.

Who They Want to Be

As you guide your teen through the process of finding their singular focus, shift the conversation from "What do you want to do?" to "Who do you want to be?" This subtle yet profound change helps them think beyond career paths and achievements and consider their character, identity, and legacy.

Encourage them to reflect on traits like kindness, perseverance, faithfulness, and integrity. Share examples of how your own character has been shaped by your experiences, and remind them that their ultimate identity is found in Christ: *"But you are a chosen people, a royal priesthood, a holy nation, God's special possession, that you may declare the praises of Him who called you out of darkness into His wonderful light"* (1 Peter 2:9).

The Teen Years: A Window of Opportunity

The teenage years represent a pivotal period in your child's development—one filled with incredible opportunities to shape their future. During adolescence, young people develop the cognitive ability to think abstractly, allowing them to envision their future selves and set long-term goals. This capacity, known as future orientation, plays a critical role in their motivation and decision-making. Teens with a strong sense of future orientation are more likely to engage in behaviors that lead to academic, personal, and professional success.

This is also a time when identity formation takes center stage. Teens start exploring who they are and what they value, building a foundation for the person they want to become. Research shows that parental involvement significantly influences this process. Parents who foster a supportive environment—providing guidance, encouragement, and opportunities for exploration—help their teens achieve a stronger sense of identity.

The teen years are a rare intersection of developmental readiness and curiosity. This is a pivotal season where vision expands, ideas flourish, and teens begin grasping how they fit into a greater story. As a parent, this is your opportunity to guide them, helping them clarify their values, discover their passions, and explore their purpose.

Why Teens Can Recognize Long-Term Goals

Contrary to the stereotype that teens are aimless, many young people have a surprisingly clear idea of what they'd like to do with their lives during this stage. Research highlights that teens who envision a positive future are more motivated to succeed academically and set meaningful goals. This clarity stems from their expanding cognitive abilities and desire to define their identity.

However, this clarity needs nurturing. Left unguided, teens can feel overwhelmed by societal pressures, the influence of peers, or the sheer number of choices they face. As a parent, your role is to help them filter out distractions and focus on what truly matters. By encouraging goal-setting and providing opportunities to explore their interests, you give them the tools to discover their singular focus.

Practical Steps for Parents

1. **Encourage Exploration:** Teens thrive when they have the freedom to explore a variety of interests and activities. Support their curiosity by introducing them to opportunities that align with their natural strengths and passions. Whether enrolling in a workshop, connecting them with mentors, or simply encouraging hobbies, these experiences can help them identify what excites them most.
2. **Facilitate Goal Setting:** Teaching your teen how to set SMART (Specific, Measurable, Achievable, Relevant, Time-bound) goals can build their confidence and

give them a sense of direction. Goal-setting fosters self-efficacy, teaching them that they have the ability to achieve what they set out to do.

3. **Model Purposeful Living:** Your teen constantly observes you, whether you realize it or not. Show them what it looks like to live with a singular focus by prioritizing your own values and passions. When they see you living intentionally, it reinforces the importance of aligning actions with purpose.
4. **Help Them Reflect on Their Identity:** Engage your teen in meaningful conversations about their values, passions, and long-term goals. Ask questions like, "What do you think is most important in life?" or "What kind of difference do you want to make in the world?" These discussions help refine their understanding of who they are and what they want to become.
5. **Support Their Spiritual Growth:** Remind your teen that their ultimate identity is found in Christ. Encourage them to seek God's guidance in discovering their purpose, knowing that He has a unique plan for their life. Model what a deepening personal relationship with Christ looks like. Let them see it in you and be drawn to duplicate.

By stepping into this critical role as a parent, you're helping your teen lay a foundation for a life of purpose, clarity, and focus. These years are a gift—an incredible opportunity to shape their future and how they see themselves and the world around them.

Final Thought

When your teen embraces singularity, they gain clarity, purpose, and confidence. They learn to say "yes" to what aligns with their values, and "no" to distractions that pull them off course. But singularity doesn't just impact their future; it transforms their present. As they focus on what matters most, they experience the joy and fulfillment of living with intention.

As a parent, you are your child's greatest cheerleader and guide. Your faith in them, paired with God's unchanging promises, will give them the courage to step boldly into their purpose. Remember, this journey isn't just about shaping your teen—it's also about how God is using this season to shape you.

Reflection Questions for Parents

1. What activities or topics does your teen naturally gravitate toward?
2. When have you seen your teen light up with joy or purpose?
3. What strengths or talents have you observed in your teen?
4. What values does your teen already demonstrate in their everyday choices?
5. What might your teen need to say "no" to to protect their purpose and peace?
6. Where do you sense God might narrow your teen's path to reveal their calling more clearly?
7. If your teen had a "North Star," what would it be?
8. How can you affirm and support their singular focus this week?

SPARK

TWO

PERSISTENCE: STAYING THE COURSE WHEN YOUR TEEN WANTS TO QUIT

Carter's Story: Ten More Minutes

In *SPARK for Emerging Leaders*, Arthur shares the story of Carter, a teen overwhelmed by academic pressure and tempted to give up. His struggle with biology class feels impossible, and rather than push through the frustration, he turns to the comfort of a video game and mentally checks out.

But Carter's story doesn't end there. When his dad notices the signs of defeat—a textbook discarded, a silent room, a glowing Xbox—he invites Carter to do something unexpected: take a walk. Not a lecture. Not a punishment. Just a quiet walk, father and son.

As they walk through their neighborhood, Carter's dad shares a story from his own teenage years—a failed attempt at learning the guitar. Like Carter, he gave up when things got hard. But a timely word from an uncle reframed everything: *"Of course it's hard. If it were easy, everyone would do it. The only difference between you and a great guitar player is that they didn't quit."*

That one insight sparked a small but steady change. Carter's dad committed to practicing ten minutes a day, no matter how bad he sounded. Over time, those ten-minute efforts added up to real progress—and eventually, passion. Years later, music became one of his greatest joys.

Back at home, Carter picked up his biology book. He didn't suddenly love the subject; it wasn't magically easier. But he set a timer—just ten minutes. And he chose persistence over avoidance for the first time in a long time.

Ask your teen what they saw in Carter's story. Where do they feel like giving up? What frustrates or intimidates them? What might ten more minutes look like in that area of life?

Persistence is often less about heroic willpower and more about showing up again, especially when it's hard. As parents, we sometimes want to fix the problem or eliminate the struggle. But the greatest gift we can give our children is the ability to keep going, even when it's uncomfortable. Sometimes all they need is a walk, a story, and someone who believes they can push through.

The Bible reminds us: *"Let us not grow weary of doing good, for at the proper time we will reap a harvest if we do not give up"* (Galatians 6:9).

Carter's story reminds us that grit is not about perfection—it's about refusing to quit. Ten more minutes today, ten more tomorrow. That's where growth happens. That's how character is built.

Help your teen name an area where they need to persevere. Encourage them to take one small step—and then another—just ten more minutes.

Steadfast persistence isn't always dramatic—it's often found in the simple act of not giving up today.

Teaching Our Teens to Stay the Course

As parents, it can be excruciating to watch our children flounder. We want to jump in, fix it, and rescue them. But what they need most isn't a shortcut to comfort—it's an invitation to keep going when quitting is easier.

We don't need to solve every problem for them. We need to show them how to keep showing up, especially when it's hard and thankless, and it feels like no progress is happening. This is where true greatness is formed.

Our kids will face moments that stretch them academically, socially, emotionally, and spiritually. They'll want to quit—some already have—but as their parent or guardian, you have the privilege of stepping in—not to rescue but to remind.

Remind them that struggle doesn't mean failure, that resilience is learned, and that God does His best work through our persistence. Romans 5:3–4 says, "*We rejoice in our sufferings, knowing that suffering produces endurance, and endurance produces character, and character produces hope.*" Isn't that what we want for our kids? It is not a smooth path, but it has a strong character—not a perfect record, but holy perseverance.

"Now, I want my kids to know that problems are a way of life. I don't like it either, but that's the way life is."

Charlie "Tremendous" Jones, *The Key to Excellence*

Adaptability Is Greater Than Ability

One of the greatest gifts we can give our teens is the understanding that resilience outperforms intelligence over the long haul. We live in a world that prizes IQ and personality. But as adults, we know better. Over time, the people who rise are not always the smartest or most charming—they are the ones who can get knocked down and get back up again.

That's the power of adaptive capacity—the ability to change, bounce back, recalibrate, and respond with strength.

Psychologists call it AQ: the Adaptability Quotient. Some say it's even more important than IQ or EQ (emotional intelligence). Why? Because life is change. And those who thrive are not those with all the answers, but those who can persist through ambiguity, setbacks, and failure.

This is a message your teen needs to hear—from you. When your teen wants to quit after one rough game, one failed test, one breakup, or one rejection, you can gently say:

"It's okay to be tired. It's okay to be discouraged. But it's not okay to give up on yourself."

Your Role in Coaching Persistence

You can't make your child persist, but you can model it, coach it, and cultivate the soil so that persistence grows.

Tell Them Your "Ten More Minutes" Stories

- Let your teen see how you've pushed through obstacles—big or small. Whether you've finished your education, dealt with workplace drama, or stayed faithful in a hard season of life, your persistence tells them what's possible. Be honest about your failures, too. Show them how you kept going even when you didn't feel strong. Your story gives them permission to struggle and the strength to carry on.

Redefine Failure Together

- Help your teen understand that failure is an event, not an identity. Say things like:
  - "You failed at something. That doesn't make you a failure."
  - "What did this mistake teach you?"
  - "What can we do differently next time?" The difference between stuck and strong is perspective.

Call Out the Culture of Quitting

- Talk about the messages your teen sees online and in school. Things like:
  - "If it's not fun, don't do it."
  - "You should only chase what lights you up."
  - "If you're not instantly good at it, it's not for you."
    These may sound empowering, but they're dangerous when taken as truth. Teach your teen that greatness comes through discipline, not just desire.

Bring Scripture into the Conversation

- Use biblical models to show what persistence really looks like:
  - Moses returned to Pharaoh over and over again.
  - Job holding to faith through unimaginable suffering.
  - Paul writing letters from prison.
  - Jesus, sweating blood in Gethsemane, choosing to carry the cross.

And don't forget the Persistent Widow (Luke 18:2–5)—even an unjust judge gave in because she refused to quit. God honors perseverance.

> **"The more I'd wanted to quit, the more I would want to quit; and the more I would want to quit, the more I was afraid I was going to quit; and I didn't want to quit, I just wanted to want to quit! And one day I learned that there's a difference between quitting and wanting to quit. What did I do? I decided I'll never, never, never, never quit, and since then I've been able to enjoy wanting to quit because I know I'm not going to quit!"**
>
> Charlie "Tremendous" Jones, *The Price of Leadership*

Spiritual Resilience: Where Persistence Truly Lives

Persistence is not just psychological. It is deeply spiritual. Scripture is full of gritty, God-fueled perseverance:

- Moses, standing up to Pharaoh again and again (Exodus 5–12).
- Paul, writing letters from prison while facing beatings and betrayal (2 Corinthians 11:24–28, Philippians 1:12–14).
- Job, enduring loss, yet holding fast to faith (Job 13:15).
- Jesus, walking toward the cross despite every opportunity to turn away (Luke 9:51, Luke 22:42, Hebrews 12:2).

Why didn't they quit? They were relying on God's power instead of willpower. Galatians 6:9 may be the most practical parenting advice of all time.

Because your teen won't just learn from your pep talks—they'll learn from your walk. Keep sowing. Keep praying. Keep showing up. Even when you feel invisible. Even when progress seems slow. God is working behind the scenes—and in your teen's heart.

When Your Teen Hits a Wall

They will. And when they do, they'll likely say things like:

- "I can't do this."
- "What's the point?"
- "I'll never be good at it."

Here's how you can respond with truth and grace:

- "That's how learning feels. You're not broken—you're growing."

- "You don't need to be perfect. You need to keep going."
- "I don't expect instant results. I respect consistent effort."

You can also ask, "What's one small step you can take today?" Not everything needs to be done now, but quitting doesn't need to be the answer.

Practical Steps for Parents

Model Consistency Over Perfection

- Let your teen see you follow through on the hard stuff. Show up to that workout. Finish that boring task. Say, "This isn't fun, but I'm doing it anyway."

Encourage the Effort, Not Just the Outcome

- Instead of "Great job on the A!" say, "I saw how hard you studied. That shows real growth." We're raising humans, not highlight reels.

Build Rhythms, Not Just Rules

- Help your teen build habits: ten minutes of reading, daily gratitude, and a consistent bedtime. Small disciplines yield big dividends over time.

Talk About What They're Learning—Not Just Doing

- Ask, "What did you learn from that challenge?" or "What surprised you about how you handled it?" These questions shift the focus from result to growth.

Encourage Regenerative Routines

- Help your teen understand that God made us to heal, restore, and renew. Physically, mentally, and spiritually, we are designed to bounce back with rest, faith, and support.

Talk About Grace-Driven Grit

- Persistence doesn't mean burnout. Teach your teen that it's okay to rest—but not to retreat from growth.

When To Push, When to Pause

Sometimes, persistence means pushing through. Other times, it means pressing pause to re-evaluate and realign.

Help your teen learn the difference:

- Is this a quitting moment or a pivoting moment?
- Am I tired, or am I called to something new?
- Am I walking away out of fear or walking toward faith?

Your job isn't always to push harder. Your job is to help them discern and then cheer them on as they take the next step.

The Long Game of Growing Strong

Don't be discouraged if your teen doesn't "get it" right away. Persistence is formed over time through a thousand little choices. The power of "just ten more minutes" can snowball into a life of faithfulness, focus, and strength.

And your voice matters deeply. Even if they roll their eyes. Even if they don't seem to be listening. Even if you feel like you've said it all before, keep showing up. Keep affirming. Keep pointing to the One who gives strength when ours runs out. "*Let us not grow weary of doing good, for in due season we will reap, if we do not give up*" (Galatians 6:9).

"You know who's 'killing their baby' today? The parent who is raising his kid to think the world is going to give him a hug and a kiss every time he turns around."

Charlie "Tremendous" Jones, *Life is Tremendous*

A Tremendous Legacy

One of the greatest lessons I ever learned came from my father, Charlie "Tremendous" Jones. In his speeches—and in our home—he would often say:

"Make a decision. Make it yours. And die by it."

Those words weren't just rhetoric. They were a way of life. From an early age, I understood that quitting was not an option. No matter how many things went wrong, no matter how discouraged I became, there was always a way to finish what I started.

My father's philosophy taught me that decisions require ownership. You don't just *try* something—you *commit* to it. You don't just drift with circumstances—you *plant your flag* in conviction and ride out the storms with grit, faith, and tremendous persistence.

This mindset shaped everything in my life:

- How I approached challenges
- How I treated setbacks
- How I trusted God to provide a way forward even when the road was hard

It's this very spirit we are called to pass on to our teens. Not a spirit of fear. Not a spirit of flakiness. But a spirit of *faithfulness*.

> *All you need to say is simply 'Yes' or 'No';*
> *anything beyond this comes from the evil one.*
> (Matthew 5:37)

In a culture where quitting is easy and commitment is rare, your voice as a parent matters more than ever. Model steadfastness.

Celebrate persistence. Teach your teen that greatness is never found on the easy path—it's forged on the narrow one. When God calls you, He equips you. And when you commit your way to Him, He will carry you through.

Final Thought

Persistence doesn't mean pretending it's easy. It means showing up when it's not. As your teen learns to persist, you're not just shaping their work ethic—you're strengthening their soul. And through it all, you're modeling what it looks like to walk by faith, not by ease.

You don't need to have all the answers. You just need to be present. Keep asking the questions, keep praying the prayers, and keep walking with them.

And remember, you're not doing this alone. The same God who strengthens your teen is strengthening you too.

Reflection Questions for Parents

1. When has your teen shown persistence—even in small ways? How can you affirm that?
2. In what areas of life does your teen seem most likely to give up?
3. How have you modeled persistence in your own life—through faith, work, health, or family?
4. What "lies about quitting" is your teen hearing from culture or peers?
5. How can you gently redirect your teen when they face frustration or failure?
6. How is God growing your own perseverance in this parenting season?
7. Where does your teen need to know, "You can try again"?
8. How are you reinforcing that their value is not tied to performance but to purpose?

SPARK

THREE

ADVOCATES: HELPING YOUR TEEN BUILD A SUPPORT SYSTEM THAT FUELS THEIR FAITH, CONFIDENCE, AND GROWTH

Wendy's Story: A Simple Invite, A Sacred Shift

In *SPARK for Emerging Leaders*, Arthur shares the story of Wendy, a quiet teen who had grown used to navigating life on her own. Her mother worked multiple jobs, and while home life was built on hard work and good intentions, it often felt empty. Wendy had learned not to expect connection, community, or closeness. Instead, she operated like a shadow, drifting through her days unnoticed and uninvited.

That changed one weekend when a classmate, Emma, invited her to a sleepover.

What may have seemed like a small gesture turned out to be a sacred turning point. In Emma's home, Wendy encountered something unfamiliar—warmth, laughter, family meals, and most notably, a sense of belonging. The next morning, Emma's family invited her to church, and to her own surprise, Wendy accepted.

That Sunday's message was about community and the truth that we weren't created to go through life alone. The words pierced through Wendy's quiet ache and awakened something deeper—a longing not just for companionship, but for people who would see her, believe in her, and call her forward.

In the days that followed, Wendy decided she wouldn't walk alone anymore. She intentionally reached out to Emma, to a caring teacher, to an older cousin, and even to her mom, despite the chaos of their schedules. One by one, she gathered a circle of Advocates: people who encouraged her, spoke life into her, and reminded her that she mattered. She began attending youth group, saw improvement in her schoolwork, and started engaging in life with a newfound confidence.

Ask your teen what stood out in Wendy's story. Who in their life serves as an Advocate right now? Who lifts them, points them to God, and challenges them to grow? And just as importantly, who are *they* becoming an Advocate for?

Wendy's journey is a powerful reminder that Advocates don't always wear capes. Sometimes they come in the form of a friend, a teacher, a family member, or even someone new who pays attention. Advocates show up. They invite. They speak truth. And they stay.

> *Two are better than one, because they have a good return for their labor: If either of them falls down, one can help the other up. But pity anyone who falls and has no one to help them up.*
> (Ecclesiastes 4:9–10)

As a parent, you play a dual role. You are likely your teen's longest-standing Advocate—but you're also their coach, helping them recognize and pursue other healthy, godly relationships.

Remind them that asking for help isn't weakness—it's wisdom. And teach them how to spot true Advocates, who sharpen their thinking, align with their values, and point them toward purpose and peace.

A simple invitation can change everything. And for teens like Wendy, it often does.

Being Your Child's Fiercest Advocate

Sometimes, being an Advocate isn't soft—it's *fierce*. There are moments when encouragement must turn into protection. As a parent, you are not just your child's cheerleader—you are their spiritual defender.

You are the one God has entrusted to guard your child's mental, emotional, physical, and spiritual health. That means you may have to speak up when others are silent, say, "This is not okay," and step into uncomfortable spaces with righteous courage and love to protect your child from people, systems, content, or relationships that could cause harm.

You are not overreacting. You are not too much. You are *appointed*.

Place a spiritual "No Trespassing" sign around your child. Guard their heart, their body, and their identity with boldness and prayer. Advocate with compassion—but also with conviction.

Jesus had this to say about those who would harm children:

> *If anyone causes one of these little ones—those who believe in me—to stumble, it would be better for them to have a large millstone hung around their neck and to be drowned in the depths of the sea.*
> (Matthew 18:6)

That's not metaphorical language. That's the protective heart of a Savior speaking to the sacredness of your child's soul. You might be the only voice standing in the gap. And even if you are—you are enough. With God's help, you are more than enough.

Why Advocates Matter

You may be the most present, prayerful, and powerful voice in your teen's life—but you aren't meant to be the only one. Our kids need more than us. And we need more than ourselves.

> *Two are better than one... A cord of*
> *three strands is not quickly broken.*
> (Ecclesiastes 4:9–12)

Whether you're parenting a thriving teen or one who's struggling, your child needs a tribe—people who show up, speak truth, and stand in the gap when your voice goes unheard. These are Advocates—and every teen (and parent) needs them. When your voice grows weary and your child tunes you out, a trusted Advocate may speak the same truth in a way that lands. Advocacy provides reinforcement, not replacement.

What Is An Advocate?

An Advocate is someone who sees greatness in your child and actively helps draw it out. They are consistent, committed, and emotionally invested in your teen's growth. True Advocates don't just show up for the wins, they walk with your child through the setbacks.

They:

- Encourage when your teen feels defeated
- Challenge when your teen needs growth
- Guide when your teen feels lost
- Correct when your teen steps off track
- Celebrate when your teen succeeds

Advocates are coaches, teachers, pastors, neighbors, youth leaders, family members, friends, mentors—and yes, sometimes strangers placed by divine appointment. Advocates don't replace your voice. They reinforce it. Their wisdom echoes your values, often confirming lessons you've already tried to teach. And when chosen wisely, they can help launch your teen toward lasting greatness.

The Power of Others

Your teen was never meant to navigate life alone, and neither were you. Advocates are people who come alongside them to offer wisdom, encouragement, and guidance (more on this in Chapter 4). This could be a teacher, a coach, a youth pastor, or even a trusted family member. Proverbs reminds us: "*Plans fail for lack of counsel, but with many advisers, they succeed*" (Proverbs 15:22).

From a very early age, your teen has been forming ideas about what leadership looks like, whether they realize it or not. According to Implicit Leadership Theory (ILT), children begin creating cognitive representations of leadership as early as ages three or four. These early impressions—shaped by their experiences with parents, teachers, coaches, friends, and even the media—serve as a blueprint for how they perceive and respond to leadership throughout their lives.

As a parent, you are the primary data point in this process. Your words, actions, and attitudes set the tone for their understanding of leadership. However, this role is shared with others, including the authority figures and peers they encounter along the way. Every interaction leaves an imprint, influencing their beliefs about what it means to lead and be led. This is why it's so important to surround your child with advocates who model integrity, humility, and Christ-like character.

The principle is simple: "trash in, trash out; spark in, spark out." What they see, hear, and experience shapes their leadership framework. If they're surrounded by negativity, cynicism, or poor examples, those influences may distort their understanding of leadership. But when they are exposed to positive, God-centered examples, it plants seeds of greatness that can bear fruit for years to come.

Help your teen recognize the positive role models already in their lives and encourage them to seek out mentors who inspire and challenge them. Likewise, be intentional about the ways you model leadership in your home. Let your child see you living out your faith, respecting others, and leading with humility and purpose. Together, these experiences will help them develop a healthy and God-honoring view of what it means to lead and follow.

What Research Tells Us About Real Advocates

According to mentoring and adolescent development research:

- Advocates provide both instrumental (practical) and emotional support
- They are present, reliable, and trustworthy
- They balance challenges with care
- They offer encouragement but also accountability

What makes a true Advocate isn't just proximity—it's intentionality. Real Advocates:

- Show up when it's inconvenient
- Speak truth when it's uncomfortable
- Believe in your teen when they've stopped believing in themselves

A healthy Advocate isn't afraid to say the hard thing with love or to set boundaries when needed. They're a mirror and a motivator, helping your teen see who they are and who they're becoming.

Why Your Teen May Resist Them (And Why You Might Too)

Here's the reality: Teens often resist outside voices—until they're ready. And let's be honest: sometimes, as parents, we resist outside voices too—especially if we feel insecure, overworked, protective, or burned by the past.

But parenting with Advocates requires humility. It means releasing some control and trusting God to use others to bless our child. You can't parent your teen in a vacuum. The challenges they're facing—identity confusion, digital overload, academic pressure, and spiritual drift—are real and relentless. They need more than your best intentions. They need godly reinforcements.

That's not weakness. That's wisdom.

The Power of Proximity: Who's Shaping Your Teen?

Arthur introduced teens to the Proximity Principle—the idea that *"we become like the people we spend the most time with."*

Let's turn that principle toward you as a parent:

- Who is shaping your teen when you're not in the room?
- Whose values are they absorbing through social media, peer groups, entertainment, or influencers?
- And what can you do to help intentionally shape their circle?

Influence happens passively and actively. It's not just who we choose—it's who we permit to remain.

It's your job to ensure their passive influences aren't louder than their purposeful ones. Whether you realize it or not, your teen is becoming someone. And who they are becoming is deeply connected to who they're becoming like.

How To Help Your Teen Build Their Advocate Network

You don't need a formal mentorship program or a perfect strategy. Start with small, intentional moments.

1. **Start With a Conversation**
   Ask your teen:
   - "Who do you feel really gets you?"
   - "Is there someone you admire at school, church, or in the family?"
   - "Who encourages you when you're discouraged?"

   Don't force it. Just ask. Plant seeds.
2. **Invite People into Their Life**
   You don't need to manufacture fake friendships. Just create intentional space:
   - Invite a trusted adult to join you for dinner
   - Ask a mentor to reach out with encouragement
   - Encourage your teen to attend youth group, a small group, or serve at church

   Make introductions—but let relationships grow naturally. Trust God with the connection.
3. **Model It Yourself**
   Show your teen what it looks like to seek wise counsel. Let them hear you say things like:
   - "I asked my mentor to pray with me about this."
   - "A friend gave me some really helpful advice."
   - "I was stuck, and I called someone I trust."

   When you normalize community and counsel, your teen will learn to value it, too.
4. **Teach Them to Identify Godly Counsel**
   Help your teen ask:
   - "Does this person lead me closer to Christ?"

- "Do they speak truth, even when it's hard to hear?"
- "Are they consistent, kind, wise, and trustworthy?"

For lack of guidance a nation falls, but
victory is own through many advisers.
(Proverbs 11:14)

Your teen's future depends on who's speaking into it.

Your Role as the Advocate Architect

As a parent, you're the Advocate Architect—not just for your teen but for your whole household. That means:

- Curating the voices your teen is exposed to
- Guarding their heart by guarding their community
- Praying for divine connections to strengthen their soul

Don't just hope your teen stumbles upon wise counsel. Help them find it and teach them to value it.

And, remind them often: you are their first Advocate. But they were never meant to walk alone.

Advocacy Is Spiritual

The greatest Advocate your child will ever have is already with them: **The Holy Spirit.**

And I will ask the Father, and He will give you another
Advocate to help you and be with you forever.
(John 14:16)

Teach your teen that they are never truly alone. The Spirit is their Guide, Convictor, Comforter, and Constant. He is the whisper in the quiet, the strength in the struggle, and the fire in their soul.

And you, parent, have the honor of modeling godly advocacy by reflecting Christ in your consistency, compassion, and courage.

Advocacy Is Also Contagious

Your teen isn't just a recipient—they're called to be a giver too. 1 Timothy 4:12 says: *"Don't let anyone look down on you because you are young, but set an example for the believers in speech, in conduct, in love, in faith, and in purity."* Even while they are being poured into, they can pour into others. Encourage them to:

- Show kindness to the lonely
- Speak up for those who are struggling
- Be a consistent, godly friend

When teens see they can be Advocates, too, they begin to take ownership of their character and community.

Teach Your Teen to Ask for Help

One of the most powerful tools your teen can carry into adulthood is the courage to ask for help. Advocated LOVE to provide help to others. This giving is one of their giftings from God. Be sure and let your teen know that these earth angels live to bless others. Encourage them to ASK and let them know:

- It's not weakness—it's wisdom
- Advocates love to bless others
- Most adults are honored to be asked for guidance, input, or mentorship

Even Jesus said, *"Ask, and it will be given to you…"* (Matthew 7:7). Asking is a principle of the kingdom—it shows humility, honors the wisdom of others, and unlocks doors that pride keeps shut. Remind your teen: *"If any of you lacks wisdom, let him ask God..."* (James 1:5). That same truth applies to earthly advocates. Most adults are honored to be asked for input. *"In an abundance of counselors there is safety"* (Proverbs 11:14).

Some teens are afraid to ask for help. Others don't even know where to start.

Your job is to normalize asking. Model it in your own life. Celebrate when they do it.

Say things like:

- "I'm proud of you for reaching out to your teacher."
- "It's wise to ask questions before starting something new."
- "Asking for help isn't a weakness—it's wisdom in motion."

Teach your teen that most people love being asked to help. It affirms their value. Advocates are often waiting to bless—they just need an invitation. Help them learn the language of initiative: "Could I ask your advice?" or "Would you help me think this through?" These simple questions unlock influence and build confidence.

Build A Team Across Every Area

One of the greatest skills you can help your teen develop is the wisdom to build a diverse, trusted team of Advocates—people they can turn to for guidance, encouragement, and perspective. Encourage your teen to seek support in every sphere of life:

- Spiritual: pastors, youth leaders, small group mentors
- Academic: teachers, tutors, guidance counselors
- Athletic: coaches, trainers, teammates
- Personal: family members, trusted friends, neighbors
- Vocational: mentors in business, trades, or leadership

Listen to advice and accept instruction,
and in the end you will be wise.
(Proverbs 19:20)

No single person can meet every need. That's not a weakness—it's a design. Different Advocates bring different strengths, wisdom, and giftings. One may offer deep listening. Another sharp accountability. One may unlock a creative solution. Another may open a door of opportunity.

You were never meant to walk alone—and neither is your teen. Teach them to draw a handful of people into their inner circle and to draw from them freely. A well-rounded support system becomes like a *spiritual advisory board*, helping your teen grow with clarity, integrity, and confidence.

You might say to them: "*You don't need to know everything—you just need to know someone who does, and have the courage to ask.*" And remind them: The strongest leaders are those who know how to lean on others wisely and choose their counsel carefully.

Practical Steps for Parents

Write Out Their Current Circle

- List the people who spend the most time with your teen. Do they build up or break down? Encourage or discourage? Guide or mislead?

Identify Gaps

- Is your teen missing a spiritual voice, a leadership model, or a peer who's walking closely with God?

Pray Specifically for Advocates

- Ask God to place the right people in your teen's life—and to remove harmful influences.

Encourage Consistent Contact

- The power of an Advocate grows over time. Help your teen schedule regular check-ins with trusted mentors.

Give Space, But Stay Present

- Sometimes teens open up more to others than to us—and that's okay. Your job isn't to control the connection. It's to bless it, nurture it, and stay supportive.

Final Thoughts

You are your teen's first Advocate. But you were never meant to be their only one.

Parenting with purpose means opening the door for other voices to walk alongside yours—voices that echo God's truth, reinforce your values, and expand your teen's view of what's possible.

Don't just build your child's résumé. Build their support system.

While skills can help them advance, Advocates will help them stay the course. And together, you'll walk with them—not just toward success, but toward *godly greatness*.

Reflection Questions for Parents, Guardian, Mentors, And Caregivers

1. Who are the key voices shaping your teen right now?
2. What areas of growth does your teen need support in—spiritually, emotionally, academically, and socially?
3. Who are 1–2 people you could intentionally bring into your teen's life to help encourage or guide them?
4. How have you seen the Proximity Principle play out in your teen's choices or personality?

5. Are there influences (online or in person) that need to be removed or limited?
6. How can you continue to model the value of wise counsel and godly community?
7. How can you pray more specifically for the right Advocates to walk with your teen this year?
8. How can your teen pour into someone else—even while they're still growing?

SPARK

FOUR

RESOURCES: HELPING YOUR TEEN INVENTORY, ACCESS, AND ACTIVATE WHAT THEY NEED TO THRIVE

Blake's Story: The Two-Column Breakthrough

In *SPARK for Emerging Leaders*, Arthur shares the story of Blake, a high school senior who feels paralyzed as graduation approaches. While his peers are celebrating college acceptances and career plans, Blake is overwhelmed by uncertainty. It's not that he doesn't care—he simply doesn't know where to begin. The process of pursuing the next steps feels confusing, discouraging, and out of reach.

Out of quiet desperation, Blake meets with his school's guidance counselor, Mrs. Packard. What follows is a simple, yet profound exercise in clarity. She draws two columns on a blank sheet of paper: *What You Already Have* and *What You Still Need.* At first, Blake insists he doesn't have anything to work with—but as they talk, the list grows.

A strong GPA. A part-time job that demonstrates responsibility. Teachers who believe in him. A supportive youth pastor. A cousin in the trades. A car. A smartphone. A caring family. Each item slowly reframes Blake's mindset. He doesn't lack potential—he just hasn't seen the full picture.

Mrs. Packard helps him build a realistic list of what's still needed: guidance on the next steps, financial aid resources, a résumé, and someone to walk him through the process. She doesn't hand him all the answers, but she does equip him with direction—and perhaps more importantly, she helps him see what he already has.

Ask your teen what stood out in Blake's story. Do they ever feel behind or overwhelmed? Are they struggling to recognize the resources around them, both material and relational?

Blake's story reminds us that many teens don't need more brilliance—they need more awareness.

They're not waiting on a miracle—they're waiting on someone to help them see what's already available and how to use it. That's where you come in.

As a parent, you are a powerful resource in your teen's life, but your deeper role is helping them recognize and steward *their* resources—not just the obvious ones like grades or gadgets, but the people, opportunities, experiences, and skills they already possess.

> *And my God will meet all your needs according to his glorious riches in Christ Jesus.*
>
> (Philippians 4:19)

When our teens feel like they've missed the boat, we remind them they're still on the dock—and many vessels are ready to set sail. Help your child create their own two-column list. You might be surprised by just how much they already have—and just how far they can go with it.

Why Resources Matter

Your teen may be motivated. They may even have a clear sense of purpose. But without resources—tools, people, support systems—they're like a slingshot stretched back with no way to launch. Vision minus provision equals frustration.

This chapter is about helping your teen identify what they already have, discover what they still need, and develop the confidence to ask for help. The world tells them to hustle harder. God tells us to steward what's already in our hands.

Resources matter because potential alone won't move your teen forward. They need traction—and traction requires tools. Think of resources like the fuel in the tank. No matter how gifted the driver or how shiny the car is, it won't move without fuel.

You Can't Launch Without Supplies

As a parent, you've probably experienced the frustration of watching your teen flounder—not because they're lazy or indifferent, but because they're under-equipped. This perceived allocation is what leadership research calls means efficacy—a person's belief that their resources are enough to accomplish their goal.

No matter how much self-belief your teen has, if they don't have the tools—or can't recognize them—they will stall. That's where you come in. A well-timed suggestion, fresh eyes, or simply naming what's already in their life can make a huge difference. You don't have to solve every problem, but your insight can clear away the fog.

The Role of the Parent as a Resource Detective

Parents are often the ones who can see what their teens can't. We can see the supportive teacher, the helpful coach, the internship opportunity, and the extra laptop lying unused in a closet.

Your job is not to do the work for them—but to help them inventory their toolbox and teach them how to ask for what they need.

Start by engaging in everyday conversations. Instead of asking, "How was school?" try, "What was one challenge today, and what could help you face it better tomorrow?" Look for moments to mention the people, programs, and provisions God has already placed in their lives.

This includes:

- People (mentors, tutors, friends, youth leaders)
- Technology (Wi-Fi, apps, computers)
- Programs (school resources, faith communities, scholarships)
- Daily needs (healthy meals, transportation, study space)
- Emotional support (counseling, encouragement, advocacy)

You may be surprised by how many are already present—and underutilized.

A Biblical View Of Resources

God is the ultimate Provider. Resources are finite in our hands—but when we place them in God's hands, they become infinite. What we see as limited, He multiplies. What we think is barely enough, He uses to overflow. Throughout Scripture, we see Him supply exactly what His people need:

- Manna in the Wilderness (Exodus 16) God provided daily bread from heaven for the Israelites during their journey through the desert.
- Water from the Rock (*Exodus 17:1–7* also *Numbers 20:1–13*) God told Moses to strike a rock, and water miraculously flowed to quench the people's thirst.
- Ravens Feeding Elijah (*1 Kings 17:1–6*) During a drought, God sent ravens to bring Elijah bread and meat, while he drank from a brook.

- A Boy's Lunch Feeding 5,000 (*John 6:1–14*) Jesus multiplied five loaves and two fish to feed a crowd, using what a child was willing to give.
- Wisdom for Solomon (*1 Kings 3:5–14*) Solomon asked God for wisdom, and God provided abundantly—giving him wisdom, wealth, and honor.
- Provision for the Widow of Zarephath (*1 Kings 17:7–16*) In a time of famine, God sustained a widow and her household with flour and oil that never ran out.

Your teen's needs are not a surprise to God. He has already positioned people, opportunities, and provisions in their lives—it's our job to help them see this and trust Him in the process.

Give us this day our daily bread...
(Matthew 6:11)

The Power of Inventorying

Arthur's guidance counselor in Blake's story made a simple but profound move: she had him list what he already had and what he still needed. You can do the same with your teen:

- Sit down together with a piece of paper
- Make two columns: "What I Have" and "What I Need"
- Fill them in with honesty, clarity, and hope

This shift moves your teen from overwhelmed to ownership. Encourage your teen to name even small things: "I have a notebook and pen," or "I know one teacher who cares." These details matter. Inventorying cultivates awareness, and awareness breeds gratitude—and strategy.

When They Think They Have Nothing

Sometimes, your teen will say, "I don't have anything." That's rarely true. Here's how to respond:

- "Let's look at what's already in your life that could help."
- "God rarely gives us everything up front—but He always gives us a starting point."
- "What's one step you could take today using what you already have?"

Help them recall past wins: "What helped you succeed the last time?" Show them how small resources can lead to big breakthroughs when handled well.

Help Your Teen Distinguish Between Wants and Needs

In a world of constant advertising and instant gratification, teaching your teen to tell the difference between what they want and what they truly need is a lifelong gift. It's not just about budgeting—it's about discernment, stewardship, and wisdom.

You might say:

- **A want** might be the newest laptop.
  A need might be uninterrupted time and a quiet space to write the essay that's due tomorrow.
- **A want** might be a flashy opportunity that looks good on social media.
  A need might be someone trustworthy to walk them through the steps of a college or job application.
- **A want** might be recognition.
  A need might be responsibility.

Suppose one of you wants to build a tower. Won't you first sit down and estimate the cost to see if you have enough money to complete it?
(Luke 14:28)

This is the essence of counting the cost—and making a plan. It's not about denying dreams; it's about building a life that can support them. Helping your teen pause, reflect, and evaluate what's essential equips them to:

- Spend their time and energy wisely
- Prioritize goals that align with their purpose
- Build habits of delayed gratification and long-term vision

This conversation isn't always easy—but it's transformative. It helps teens realize they don't have to chase every shiny thing to succeed. They just need the right tools, the right team, and a plan grounded in truth.

When Resources Run Dry

There will be drought seasons—spiritually, emotionally, financially. Times when what once sustained us no longer does. That doesn't mean God has left the building. In 1 Kings 17, Elijah drinks from a brook and is fed by ravens—divine provision in a time of crisis. But eventually, *even that brook dries up.* Did God abandon him? Not at all. God had already arranged the next provision: a poor widow in Zarephath who, despite her lack, became part of Elijah's miraculous journey.

The lesson? God's resources may shift—but His faithfulness never does. His methods may change, but His character does not.

Remind your teen that closed doors often lead to better ones. When one stream dries up, it's not a dead end—it's a redirect. Often, what feels like a setback is actually preparation for something new. And sometimes, the waiting in between resources is the classroom where trust is tested and deepened.

Let them know:

- Just because provision looks different doesn't mean God isn't providing.
- He may use unexpected people, places, or paths.
- When resources feel scarce, lean on the Source—not the supply.

The jar of flour was not used up and
the jug of oil did not run dry...
(1 Kings 17:16)

The lions may grow weak and hungry, but those
who seek the LORD lack no good thing.
(Psalms 34:10)

Steward What You Have—And Share It

Your teen may not realize it yet, but they are already a resource to someone else. They may not have a car, a paycheck, or a college degree—but they *do* have time, energy, creativity, and presence. And when they choose to share what they have, God uses it—not only to bless others, but to multiply it back to them.

A generous person will prosper; whoever
refreshes others will be refreshed.
(Proverbs 11:25)

In God's economy, giving is not losing—it's planting. Every act of service is a seed, and seeds always produce something more than they started with.

Encourage your teen to look for ways to serve right where they are:

- Tutor a younger student who needs encouragement or academic support
- Volunteer at church—greeting, helping in children's ministry, tech, music, or set-up
- Support a local nonprofit with hands-on help, organizing drives, or creative ideas
- Listen to a struggling friend—sometimes presence is the most powerful provision
- Share their skills—editing a video, designing a flyer, fixing something, writing a post

These aren't just good deeds—they're acts of spiritual stewardship. Remind your teen that:

- God sees every act of generosity
- Their influence grows when they serve
- Giving to others doesn't shrink their resources—it expands their capacity

The best way to develop as a leader is to act like a servant. The best way to receive more is to give what you already have.

Help them see themselves not as empty or waiting to arrive—but as already equipped to pour out. They are someone's answered prayer.

Watch For Wasted Resources

Sometimes, the issue isn't lack—it's leakage. It's not that God hasn't provided—it's that the provision is being misused, misunderstood, or simply ignored.

Teens often don't realize that neglect is a form of waste. An unused gift, a forgotten opportunity, a mishandled responsibility—all of these can drain potential and delay growth. Help your teen develop the eyes to see where resources might be slipping through the cracks.

Encourage them to ask:

- *"What am I not using that could help me right now?"*(Is there a relationship, a tool, or a habit they've been neglecting?)
- *"What am I wasting—time, energy, opportunity?"*(Are they pouring effort into distractions instead of development?)
- *"What needs to be repurposed or redirected?"*(Could that screen time become study time? Could that app become a tool instead of a trap?)

And then teach them the joy of releasing what's no longer needed. If there's a book, device, piece of clothing, or tool your family no longer uses, pass it on. What's gathering dust in your home might be the very thing someone else is praying for.

Your unused blessing may be someone else's breakthrough.

Model this in your own life, too. Clean out. Give away. Bless others freely. Living open-handedly teaches teens that generosity is not just about money—it's about movement. It's about letting resources flow through your hands instead of stagnating in them.

Because the truth is: God can't fill a hand that's clenched. But when we open our grip, He often surprises us with even more.

Resourcefulness > Resources

One of the greatest lessons you can give your teen is that resourcefulness matters more than having every resource in hand. It's not about waiting until everything is perfect—it's about learning how to work with what you have and pursue what you don't.

Being resourced is helpful. But being resourceful is powerful. Help your teen develop the mindset that says: "*I may not have everything—but I can figure out what to do next.*"

Teach them how to:

- Research tools and solutions instead of giving up when confused
- Send a professional email to request help or explore an opportunity
- Follow up with a mentor and express gratitude
- Attend workshops, trainings, or webinars—even on their own initiative
- Pray specifically—not vaguely—for what they need: wisdom, provision, connection, clarity

Use Blake's story as a reminder: He didn't gain new resources overnight—he activated what had been around him all along. He didn't need more stuff—he needed a strategy.

Remind your teen:

- You are not without options.
- You are not stuck.
- You are not alone.

Resourcefulness is a *character trait*, not a circumstance. It's the decision to look up, reach out, and move forward—even when the toolkit feels empty.

And don't forget—God is the ultimate Source. When your teen starts activating what's in front of them, heaven often opens what's ahead of them.

Final Thought

Your teen's journey toward greatness isn't about having everything in place—it's about learning to see what God has already placed around them. Help them take inventory, encourage them to take action, and remind them that they are never alone, never without options, and never without a Provider.

They don't need every tool. They just need to start with what's in their hand—and trust God for the rest.

Reflection Questions for Parents

1. What resources—people, tools, habits—do you see in your teen's life they might be overlooking?
2. When was the last time your teen asked for help? How did you respond?
3. In what ways can you model resourcefulness in front of your teen?
4. Are there any "dry wells" (drained resources) in your teen's life that need to be revisited or released?
5. How can you equip your teen this week with something practical, relational, or spiritual?

SPARK

FIVE

KNOWLEDGE: HELPING YOUR TEEN BECOME A LIFELONG LEARNER AND CRITICAL THINKER

Julie's Story: The 3L Club Conversation

In *SPARK for Emerging Leaders*, Arthur shares the story of Julie, a teenager who sees school as a burden and learning as irrelevant. While her classmates dive into the new school year with excitement, Julie approaches it with skepticism and apathy. In her view, education is a tedious exercise in memorizing useless facts, not something that will serve her in real life.

But everything shifts during a parent–teacher conference with her English teacher, Mr. Clarke.

Rather than recycle the usual phrases about "unmet potential," Mr. Clarke takes a different approach. He asks Julie if she's a member of the 3L Club. When she shrugs it off, he explains: **Life. Long. Learner.** It's not about loving school—it's about embracing the mindset that growth, curiosity, and wisdom are essential to living well.

Mr. Clarke doesn't try to sell Julie on a subject—he invites her to imagine what it would be like to approach life with the confidence that comes from learning how to learn. He affirms that she has great instincts and insightful questions, and gently challenges her to apply them with purpose.

That conversation becomes a turning point.

Later that night, Julie writes a list titled *"Stuff I Actually Want to Learn"*—a mix of life skills and real-world curiosity. From that moment on, something begins to shift. She doesn't suddenly become an academic superstar, but starts showing up differently. She listens more. She participates more. She opens her heart—and her mind.

Ask your teen what stood out in Julie's story. Do they resonate with her doubts about school? What would be on their list of things they actually want to learn?

Grades didn't fuel Julie's transformation—it was sparked by ownership. When teens begin to understand that knowledge is more than classroom achievement—that it's tied to freedom, discernment, opportunity, and wisdom—they engage with the world on a deeper level.

As parents, we want our children to succeed academically, but far more importantly, we want them to be teachable, humble, hungry learners who pursue truth and make wise decisions.

Scripture says: *"The beginning of wisdom is this: Get wisdom. Though it cost all you have, get understanding"* (Proverbs 4:7). And again: *"The heart of the discerning acquires knowledge, for the ease of the wise seek it out"* (Proverbs 18:15).

Knowledge equips our children to live boldly, think critically, and lead well. Whether they learn how to budget, discern truth from lies, write clearly, or navigate relationships, everything they take in becomes part of the foundation for the life they're building.

Encourage your teen to reflect on what they'd genuinely like to learn and what kind of person they want to become. Remind them that being smart isn't about knowing everything. It's about staying curious, asking good questions, and remaining teachable all their lives.

Because in the end, what we're after isn't perfection—it's pursuit. The humble, steady pursuit of wisdom, growth, and godly understanding. That's what it means to join the 3L Club. And that's how greatness begins.

Preparing The Soil: The Parent's Role in Cultivating a Learning Environment

In Matthew 13, Jesus tells us about the Parable of the Sower. The sower scatters seeds—some fall on rocky ground, some among thorns, and some on good soil. Only the seed that falls on good soil produces a harvest.

> *Still other seed fell on good soil, where it produced a crop—a hundred, sixty or thirty times what was sown.*
> (Matthew 13:8)

As a parent, you are not just a sower of truth and wisdom; you are also a *gardener of soil.*

Your teen may be handed great lessons, godly mentors, and biblical truth. But if their environment is filled with constant distraction, anxiety, negative peer influence, or apathy, the seed may not take root.

Creating an environment that fosters knowledge means:

- Setting rhythms of rest and quiet for reflection
- Being mindful of digital noise and mental clutter
- Modeling an open mind and a teachable spirit
- Ensuring your teen has access to Scripture, books, meaningful conversation, and healthy dialogue
- Choosing friends who have a desire to learn and achieve academic excellence

Just as a garden needs weeding, watering, sunlight, and time—so does your teen's mind. Ask, "What kind of soil am I preparing in my home?" You're not responsible for the growth. God makes things grow (1 Corinthians 3:6–7). But you *are* responsible for the soil. Protect it. Nurture it. And trust the seeds to take root in due time.

These commandments that I give you today
are to be on your hearts. Impress them on
your children. Talk about them when you sit
at home and when you walk along the road,
when you lie down, and when you get up.
(Deuteronomy 6:6–7)

"You'll be the same person five years from now that you are today except for two things: the people you meet and the books you read."

Charlie "Tremendous" Jones

If we want our teens to grow, we must help them understand the power of knowledge—not just information but *transformation.* Knowledge fuels confidence, enables critical thinking, expands perspective, and helps teens evaluate truth in a world full of noise and half-truths. And the more they learn—biblically, intellectually, emotionally—the more wisely they will live.

Indecision Is a Symptom of Ignorance

Have you watched your teen freeze when facing a decision? That's often not rebellion—it's paralysis. They don't know what they don't know—and that's terrifying. Arthur once shared a story about waiting on a promotion decision. The delay wasn't due to laziness or poor leadership—it was simply a lack of knowledge. No one moved forward because they didn't have enough information to make the call. That's what our teens face every day if we don't equip them. Don't just tell your teen to "figure it out." Teach them how to explore, how to ask, how to discern.

This is where the truth of God's sovereignty and omniscience becomes incredibly freeing. All truth is God's truth. He is the Creator of all things—every equation, every insight, every skill, every field of study. Because of that, we don't need to fear indecision. We're not expected to *know it all*—only to *seek the One who does*. When we understand that God has already seen the end from the beginning, the pressure to make the "perfect" choice is lifted. Our role is not to be omniscient—it's to be faithful. We are not the Architect—we are the Discoverers.

What a relief, even for us as adults! Our job is to do our best, seek wisdom, and take the next step. God will guide our steps, redirect when needed, and unfold His plans with perfect timing. That mindset transforms knowledge-seeking from a chore into an adventure—a discovery journey we walk with Him, hand in hand. What a tremendous way to think about gaining wisdom: not as pressure, but as partnership with the God who already knows the way.

This is the heartbeat of the 3L Club: not perfection, but pursuit. Because leadership is lifelong learning—and every faithful step we take with God is a step toward the leader He created us to become.

The Biblical Roots of True Knowledge

In a culture that preaches relativism, we must point our children back to truth as a person—Jesus Christ. Scripture doesn't just tell us what to know—it teaches us how to think.

Sanctify them by the truth; your word is truth.
(John 17:17)

Your word is a lamp for my feet and a light on my path.
(Psalms 119:105)

Start with the Proverbs. Read one a day with your teen. Discuss it. Apply it. Let them wrestle with it. There are 31 chapters, so you can cover the entire book each month—and watch how its wisdom transforms your home. (See the 31 Day Challenge on Page 85).

During my doctoral studies, one of my professors told me that the Book of Proverbs is the greatest leadership book ever written. He was right. Proverbs teaches us how to lead ourselves and others. It offers instruction on how to speak wisely, work diligently, handle debt, manage money, honor marriage, raise children, resolve conflict, and live in peace with our neighbors. It even tells us how to treat our animals! (*A righteous man cares for the needs of his animal* — Proverbs 12:10.)

Wisdom isn't just academic—it's spiritual. Proverbs isn't outdated—it's timeless. In a world that bombards our teens with half-truths and distorted values, God's Word remains the clearest guide. It shapes hearts, sharpens minds, and lights the path forward.

Adults Must Model the Desire to Grow

As parents, we often ask our teens to be curious, focused, and diligent— forgetting that we, too, must model a commitment to learning and excellence. Let's be honest: are you monitoring your own screen time? Are you filling your mind with things that sharpen your faith and renew your thinking? Or are you doom-scrolling, binge-watching, or zoning out?

Remember ILT (Implicit Leadership Theory)? The habit of reading isn't something we're born with—it's something we learn by watching others. When someone we admire models a life of curiosity and learning, it sparks that same desire in us. I've heard it said that a love of reading is first nurtured on a parent's lap as they read to their child. That's where it begins: presence, rhythm, voice, and story.

Are you sitting at the dinner table and sharing something you learned that day? Growing up, every meal was a family gathering—six kids and two adults—where we'd talk about our day, what we read, what we learned in school. We often had devotionals and reading time at the table instead of dessert!

Do you read regularly? Do you challenge yourself with new ideas? Do you allow others to teach you something? While you drive, do you listen to sermons or uplifting podcasts that shape your worldview? Let your teen see you pursuing knowledge. It will make a profound impact on them. Everything starts with the Word—spoken, written, prayed, heard, absorbed. Our homes must be centered on it.

In the beginning was the Word, and the Word
was with God, and the Word was God.

(John 1:1)

I didn't develop a true need to grow until my mid-40s. I was always book-smart and had read consistently, but my knowledge assimilation was purely transactional. I read to get the information I needed—to get paid, get promoted, to get things done. But over time, God began transforming my reason for reading. I started reading to renew my mind, soften my heart, and let Him sanctify me through truth. Now, I read to be changed—not just to be informed.

That's the shift we want our teens to make too. But we must walk the path first.

Make your home a living laboratory of learning. Share articles. Keep books visible. Watch your tone when your teen asks a question. Curiosity isn't defiance—it's a signal of desire. It's a window for discipleship.

You are still your child's most important teacher. Let them see you learning—so they never stop believing they can, too.

Reading Is a Habit—Not A Talent

Teens often say, "I'm just not a reader."

But that's like saying, "I'm just not a runner." Reading isn't a personality trait—it's a skill, a behavior, and a habit that can be developed over time. It may not come naturally at first, but with exposure, encouragement, and consistency, it can become second nature.

My father, Charlie "Tremendous" Jones, believed so deeply in the power of reading that he paid us to write book reports. This wasn't a gimmick—it was real money with real impact. He saw books as the gateway to growth, and he knew the investment was worth it.

In his bestselling book *Life Is Tremendous*, he shared a story about cultivating a love of reading in my brother, Jere. At the time, my father realized he was doing more complaining about the state of the world than leading change in his own home. So, he got intentional. He didn't force reading—he sparked desire. Here's how he described it:

> *"I—like most dads—have been critical of the way they do things in Washington, but one day I realized I was running a worse program in my home than the politicians in government. I decided it was time for a change, and since books had been so tremendously helpful in my life, I decided to use them with my son. I knew Jere would rebel against my forcing him to read, so I planned some strategy... I decided to put some salt in Jere's oats and make him thirsty.*

> *'Jere, in two years you're going to want me to help you buy a car, and I want to help you. But I'm not going to give you the money. Here is my proposal. I'm going to pay you $10 for every book you read. I'll pick the book, you give me a written report, and I'll put $10 in a car fund. So, if you read in style, you'll drive in style. But if you read like a bum, you'll drive like a bum.'*
>
> *Overnight, he developed a tremendous hunger for reading!"*

You can do the same. Set a goal: one book a month. Offer a small reward. Let your teen help choose the book—with guidance and intention. Make it a family tradition, a legacy of literacy, and leadership. I've included the reading contract in the back of this book for you to use as a template!

Because books change people. Start young. Stay consistent. Keep the spark alive. Reading isn't just for school—it's for life.

Why Critical Thinking Matters More Than Ever

Study after study confirms what employers, educators, and parents already know: critical thinking is one of the most missing—and most desperately needed—traits in today's workforce. The ability to question, evaluate, and reason is more valuable than ever, yet often underdeveloped in our teens.

They're flooded with information but often lack the tools to sift fact from fiction, bias from truth, emotion from logic. In an age of constant scrolling, viral soundbites, and algorithm-driven content, the ability to pause, reflect, compare, and conclude is not just a skill—it's a safeguard.

The good news? You don't need a philosophy degree to raise a critical thinker. You just need intentional conversations, modeling discernment, and the courage to let your teen wrestle with complexity. You can help by:

- Asking, "What do you think?" instead of jumping in with answers *(Let them process. Silence is not failure—it's forming thought.)*
- Comparing different perspectives on the same topic *("Why do you think people come to different conclusions?")*
- Teaching them to research, vet, and cite sources *(Show them how to check facts, identify bias, and trace origins.)*
- Encouraging them to respectfully challenge ideas they don't agree with *(Disagreement isn't defiance—it's development when done with grace.)*

Also—expose them to high-quality thinking. Read editorials from different viewpoints. Watch debates and analyze structure. Break down the logic of advertisements, social media trends, and movies. Teach them that **every** message comes with a motive—and every motive can be questioned with wisdom.

Above all, remember this: critical thinking starts at home. Not in a textbook, not on a debate stage—but around the table, in the car, during dinner conversations, and even in those "why?" moments that make you want to sigh. Those are golden opportunities to lead them into deeper waters.

And it starts with us—modeling humility, curiosity, and discernment.

Because our teens won't become better thinkers if they only see us as louder talkers. They'll grow when they see us listening well, asking honest questions, and admitting when we need to learn too.

Remember:

> *To answer before listening—that is folly and shame.*
>
> (Proverbs 18:13)

My dear brothers and sisters, take note of this: Everyone should be quick to listen, slow to speak, and slow to become angry.
(James 1:19)

You don't need a Ph.D. to inspire your teen. You just need to stay curious—and let them see it.

- Share what you're learning.
- Read in front of them.
- Invite them into your process—whether you're troubleshooting the dishwasher or studying Scripture.

Also, let them *teach you.* Ask them what they're reading or studying. Give them the floor. Invite them to present their ideas. Nothing builds confidence like being listened to with respect.

The Brain Loves Learning

Neurologically, our brains are designed for growth. Cognitive motivation (also called intellectual efficacy) is our internal drive to seek understanding. At age 87, Michelangelo said, "*Ancora imparo*"—I am still learning. Pablo Casals practiced cello daily in his 90s. When asked why, he replied, "I think I see improvement." Your teen doesn't need to "arrive." They just need to stay open. Learning is a sign of humility. Of maturity. Of readiness. Let your home be a place that celebrates effort, curiosity, and the sacred pursuit of knowledge.

Encourage your teen to be self-directed learners:

- Set learning goals (like learning a new skill, language, or hobby)
- Take notes during sermons or podcasts
- Write reflections on what they're discovering

Introduce them to thinkers that stretch them. Give them books "just a bit beyond them," as Oswald Chambers said. Help them rise.

Creating a Household Culture of Learning

Here's how to build a learning-rich environment at home:

Create a knowledge wall

- Let your family post what they're learning, what books they're reading, and what questions they're asking. Make learning visual and shared.

Host a book report night

- Let your teen share a short reflection on a book or podcast—and pay them for it! Make it celebratory and consistent. Even non-readers will show up for snacks and a sense of accomplishment.

Ask curiosity questions

- Around the table or in the car, go beyond "How was your day?" Ask:
  - "What surprised you today?"
  - "What's one question you wish someone would answer?"
  - "What do you want to learn before next year?"

Let hobbies teach

- Encourage hands-on learning through cooking, photography, coding, drawing, or mechanics. Every project is a chance to grow a skill—and their confidence.

Final Thought

Knowledge is more than information. It's inspiration. It's preparation. It's transformation. The more your teen learns, the more they'll grow—not just in competence but confidence and character. Show them that learning is not a task. It's a treasure.

Reflection Questions for Parents

1. How do you model learning in your home?
2. What habits around reading, curiosity, or growth are visible to your teen?
3. When did you last reward or celebrate something your teen *learned* (not just achieved)?
4. What barriers does your teen face to becoming a lifelong learner—and how can you help remove them?
5. What rhythms could you build this week to create more space for discovery?

CONCLUSION

Trevor didn't think he had what it took. Haley thought being busy meant she was on the right path. Carter wanted to give up. Wendy felt completely alone. Blake thought he had nothing going for him. Julie didn't see the point of learning.

But something changed.

Each of them discovered a SPARK—a flicker of clarity, a moment of faith, a shift in perspective. They didn't stumble upon greatness. They stepped into it, one decision, one conversation, one prayer at a time. They didn't need "molded," they needed unfolded. From the beginning of the world, God ordained the paths of each of us. Our job is to walk with Him as He reveals each step of the way.

And as parents, mentors, and guardians, *we* played a role in that transformation. This book is about more than parenting strategies. It is a call to ignite the greatness within our children by walking alongside them in spirit, truth, and intentionality.

We've explored the SPARK Framework not just as a catchy acronym but as a spiritual and practical path forward—a framework for growth, a blueprint for impact, and a guide for shaping our teens into wise, grounded, God-glorifying young men and women.

Let's walk through it one last time, this time as the *igniters and keeper of the flame.*

S — Singularity

You helped your teen discover their values, passions, and purpose. You taught them that doing more doesn't mean becoming more, that clarity beats chaos, and that God created them as one-of-a-kind masterpieces with a mission only they can fulfill.

When Haley's life became a checklist of achievements, a trusted mentor finally asked her the question none had. Singularity means choosing what matters most—and letting go of what doesn't. You've modeled that by making space for what matters in your own life, too.

We are God's handiwork, created in Christ
Jesus to do the good works, which God
prepared in advance for us to do.
(Ephesians 2:10)

P — Persistence

You taught your teen that setbacks aren't stop signs, failure isn't final, growth takes time, and progress isn't always visible.

When Carter wanted to give up, his dad reminded him that *ten more minutes* could change everything. And when your teen hits the wall, you're now ready to remind them that grit fueled by grace is what wins the day.

Let us not become weary in doing good, for at the
proper time we will reap a harvest if we do not give up.
(Galatians 6:9)

A — Advocates

Wendy's transformation started with a simple invitation. Because someone reached out, she realized she wasn't alone.

You've now seen the power of Advocates—and your power as one. You're not just parenting from the sidelines. You are speaking truth, noticing, inviting, and echoing the voice of the Holy Spirit. And you're teaching your teen to both *receive* and *become* an advocate themselves.

And I will ask the Father, and He will give you another Advocate, to help you and be with you forever.
(John 14:16)

R — Resources

Blake thought he had nothing. But with a little help, he saw that his toolbox was fuller than he realized. So is your teen's.

You've learned to help them inventory what they have, name what they need, and take bold steps to ask for help and activate opportunities. You've shown them how to use what God has already provided—and trust Him for what hasn't arrived yet.

You've also been reminded to check your own resource rhythms. Are you stewarding what you have? Are you resting? Praying? Preparing?

A generous person will prosper; whoever refreshes others will be refreshed.
(Proverbs 11:25)

K — Knowledge

Julie didn't hate learning—she hadn't yet discovered what she loved to learn. Thanks to Mr. Clarke's 3L Club, she began a new journey: one driven by curiosity, not compliance.

You've learned how to model reading, pursue truth, practice discernment, and cultivate a house of learners. You've seen how Scripture shapes thinking. And you've helped reframe your teen's understanding: that knowledge is not about perfection; it's about pursuit.

Wisdom is supreme; therefore get wisdom.
Though it cost all you have, get understanding.
(Proverbs 4:7)

The Real Power Source

Whenever something breaks, we first check the power. Is it plugged in? Is the battery charged?

The same is true for our lives. SPARK is only possible when it's plugged into the Source. Without God, knowledge becomes noise. Grit becomes burnout. Relationships become obligations. Direction becomes distraction.

But *with* God? Everything ignites.

We don't just need confidence and competence. We need conviction, care, and the courage to put our dreams, our families, and our futures squarely in the hands of the One who can multiply them.

Now unto Him who is able to do immeasurably
more than all we ask or imagine, according
to His power that is at work within us.
(Ephesians 3:20)

Partners In The Divine Nature

Through these He has given us His very great
and precious promises, so that through them
you may participate in the divine nature.
(2 Peter 1:4)

This isn't just about motivation. It's about *transformation.* And it begins when we place our SPARK in His hands. If we want our teens to embrace their inheritance, we must first claim our own. If we want to pass on the mantle of faith, we must wear it boldly ourselves.

Let them see you grow. Let them hear you pray. Let them watch you worship, stumble, recover, read, rest, lead, and learn.

That's how sparks are fanned into flames. That's how legacies are made.

God Ordains the Path—We Walk it in Faith

From the very beginning of the world, God has ordained the paths of His children. Before the foundations of the earth were laid, He saw you. He saw your child. He knew their purpose. He shaped their days. He lovingly crafted a plan that would draw them closer to Himself.

Before I formed you in the womb I knew you,
before you were born I set you apart.
(Jeremiah 1:5)

Our job as parents isn't to forge a new way. It's not to map out every turn. It's not to force outcomes. Our job is to walk with God, stay in step with the Spirit, and trust Him to reveal the next step in His perfect timing.

Your word is a lamp for my feet and a light on my path.
(Psalms 119:105)

You don't have to figure it all out in advance. Your child doesn't need to have a fully formed blueprint for their life at 14, 18, or even 28. Your family's job is to stay on the path of discovery—learning, growing, and trusting that the One who called them is faithful.

He who calls you is faithful, and He will do it.
(1 Thessalonians 5:24)

This journey isn't about frantic striving. It's about steady abiding. It's about knowing that the God who authors beginnings also authors beautiful endings.

Being confident of this, that he who began
a good work in you will carry it on to
completion until the day of Christ Jesus.
(Philippians 1:6)

You're not forging the path. You're following the One who already paved it with His love. Walk boldly. Walk joyfully. Walk faithfully.

And teach your child to do the same.

Final Charge

You are not just raising kids.
You are igniting greatness.
You are not just managing behavior.
You are modeling transformation.
So now that you have these five essential tools—Singularity, Persistence, Advocates, Resources, and Knowledge—
Name it. Claim it. Live it. Share it.
And let the fire of God within you become the fire that shapes the next generation.
Because once the spark is lit, the flame cannot be ignored.
Let's go light up the world. Together.

It has given me great joy to find some of your children walking in the truth, just as the Father commanded us.
(2 John 1:4)

Personal Reflection Questions for Parents

1. Singularity: What are you doing to model clarity of purpose and values to your teen? What are you focused on right now that they can see you living out with intentionality?
2. Persistence: Where in your life have you shown grit lately? How can you share that story with your teen to encourage their own perseverance?
3. Advocates: Who are the key voices speaking truth and wisdom into your life right now? Are you allowing others to support and challenge you?
4. Resources: What resources are already in your life that you can better activate to bless your family? Where might God be inviting you to step into more stewardship or generosity?
5. Knowledge: What are you learning right now? How are you stretching your mind and renewing your thinking with truth, Scripture, or wisdom from others?
6. How are you showing your teen that growth is a lifelong process—and that you're still on the journey with them?
7. What is one step you can take this week to strengthen your influence, your example, and your intentional investment in your teen's walk with God and their future?

SPARK BIBLICAL REFLECTIONS: A PARENT'S DEVOTIONAL COMPANION

Throughout this book, you've walked with your teen through the five traits that ignite lasting leadership—Singularity, Persistence, Advocates, Resources, and Knowledge. But long before your child ever showed signs of these traits, Scripture showed us what they look like in action. Not in grown leaders—but in children, teens, and young adults chosen and anointed by God.

This section is your devotional companion. These Biblical Reflections invite you to see SPARK in the lives of youth in Scripture—and in your own child. They remind us that God doesn't wait for adulthood to begin His work. And you don't have to wait to affirm what you see in your teen. Your encouragement, your attentiveness, and your spiritual leadership may be the very voice God uses to confirm their calling.

Use these reflections after each chapter, during your quiet time, or as prompts for journaling and prayer. Let them fuel your confidence as you guide your teen to unfold—not be molded—into who God created them to be.

Biblical Reflection – Singularity in Action

Read: Genesis 37–50
Example: Joseph, a dreamer with divine vision
Key Verse: "*You intended to harm me, but God intended it for good...*" – Genesis 50:20

Joseph's life was marked by a singular, God-given vision—even when everything around him said otherwise. Betrayed by his brothers, imprisoned unjustly, and forgotten by men, he never lost sight of what God had revealed. He stayed focused, faithful, and eventually stepped into a position of incredible influence.

Just like Joseph, your teen may have a deep internal drive or sense of purpose that others don't yet understand. This chapter will help you nurture their Singularity—trusting that clarity, not conformity, is their calling.

Biblical Reflection – Persistence in Action

Read: Daniel 1–6
Example: Daniel, exiled but unwavering
Key Verse: *"But Daniel resolved not to defile himself..."* —Daniel 1:8

Daniel was likely a teenager when taken to Babylon. Despite new surroundings, foreign customs, and political pressure, he persisted in living out his faith. Through daily discipline, prayer, and consistency, Daniel outlasted kings and adversaries alike.

Like Daniel, your child's persistence may show up in quiet ways—habits, values, or bold stances. Learn how to steward this resilience so it leads to influence, not burnout.

Biblical Reflection – Advocates in Action

Read: 2 Timothy 1:3–7; 3:14–17
Example: Timothy, nurtured by generational faith
Key Verse: *"I am reminded of your sincere faith, which first lived in your grandmother Lois and in your mother Eunice..."* – 2 Timothy 1:5

Timothy's life was shaped long before his public ministry. His mother and grandmother laid a foundation of Scripture, and Paul built upon it as a spiritual father. This layered advocacy gave Timothy confidence to lead at a young age.

As a parent, you are your child's first and fiercest advocate. This chapter will help you identify and activate the Advocates your child needs—while modeling that role yourself.

Biblical Reflection – Resources in Action

Read: 2 Kings 11–12 (Joash); 2 Kings 22–23 (Josiah)
Example: Joash and Josiah, kings crowned in youth
Key Verse: *"Because your heart was responsive and you humbled yourself before the Lord..."* – 2 Kings 22:19
Joash became king at seven. Josiah at eight. Both were given wise spiritual mentors who shaped their access to truth and justice. With godly guidance and access to Scripture, they led sweeping national reforms while still young.

Your child is being formed by the resources around them—books, voices, mentors, routines. This chapter equips you to supply the right inputs so their output can honor God.

Biblical Reflection – Knowledge in Action

Read: Luke 2:41–52
Example: Jesus at age 12
Key Verse: *"Didn't you know I had to be in my Father's house?"* – Luke 2:49
At 12, Jesus amazed temple teachers with His understanding. He wasn't merely obedient—He was intellectually and spiritually awake. His knowledge came from deep spiritual curiosity and divine identity, even in youth.

Knowledge isn't just about schoolwork—it's about spiritual hunger, curiosity, and wisdom. This chapter helps you cultivate a home where learning and leadership grow hand in hand.

31-DAY PROVERBS CHALLENGE

Growing in Wisdom Together

For each day of the month, read the corresponding chapter of Proverbs aloud or individually. Then, use the reflection prompt to spark discussion, journaling, or prayer. No need to be perfect—just be present.

Each day, ask: What did this chapter teach us about God, ourselves, and how to live wisely?

Day 1 — Proverbs 1
Theme: The Beginning of Wisdom
What does it mean to "fear the Lord"? Why is that the starting point for real knowledge?

Day 2 — Proverbs 2
Theme: Searching for Wisdom
How can we pursue wisdom the way we pursue treasure? What's something we'd be wise to search for right now?

Day 3 — Proverbs 3
Theme: Trust and Honor
"Trust in the Lord with all your heart..." Where do we struggle to trust God?

Day 4 — Proverbs 4
Theme: Guarding Your Heart
What are some practical ways to guard our hearts in daily life?

Day 5 — Proverbs 5
Theme: Integrity and Boundaries
What's the danger of ignoring wise counsel?

Day 6 — Proverbs 6
Theme: Diligence Over Laziness
What's one area of our life where we could be more diligent?

Day 7 — Proverbs 7
Theme: Avoiding Temptation
How can we recognize and resist temptation?

Day 8 — Proverbs 8
Theme: Wisdom's Call
How does wisdom speak to us in daily life?

Day 9 — Proverbs 9
Theme: Wise vs. Foolish Choices
What's a wise decision we need to make this week?

Day 10 — Proverbs 10
Theme: The Power of Words
How can our words build others up today?

Day 11 — Proverbs 11
Theme: Honesty and Generosity
What does it mean to live a life of integrity?

Day 12 — Proverbs 12
Theme: Righteous Living
What's one thing we learned today about character?

Day 13 — Proverbs 13
Theme: Discipline and Companionship
Why does who we spend time with matter so much?

Day 14 — Proverbs 14
Theme: Wisdom in Action
Where can we act more wisely today?

Day 15 — Proverbs 15
Theme: Gentle Answers and Listening
How does responding gently change a conversation?

Day 16 — Proverbs 16
Theme: God Directs Our Steps
Where do we need to trust God's direction more?

Day 17 — Proverbs 17
Theme: Peacemaking and Patience
How can we bring peace into a tense situation?

Day 18 — Proverbs 18
Theme: Listening and Humility
Why is it wise to listen before we speak?

Day 19 — Proverbs 19
Theme: Desire with Knowledge
How do we gain knowledge before rushing into decisions?

Day 20 — Proverbs 20
Theme: Honesty and Justice
What does it mean to live honorably in God's eyes?

Day 21 — Proverbs 21
Theme: Heart and Motive
How can we check our motives before acting?

Day 22 — Proverbs 22
Theme: Raising the Next Generation
What values are we modeling for others?

Day 23 — Proverbs 23
Theme: Contentment and Discipline
How can we stay focused on what really matters?

Day 24 — Proverbs 24
Theme: Strength in Adversity
How do we hold to wisdom even when life is hard?

Day 25 — Proverbs 25
Theme: Self-Control
Why is self-control a strength, not a weakness?

Day 26 — Proverbs 26
Theme: Fools and Wise Responses
When is it wise to walk away instead of argue?

Day 27 — Proverbs 27
Theme: Friendship and Accountability
What makes a true friend? How can we be one?

Day 28 — Proverbs 28
Theme: Boldness in Righteousness
Where do we need to take a stand for what's right?

Day 29 — Proverbs 29
Theme: Leadership and Justice
What can we learn about godly leadership today?

Day 30 — Proverbs 30
Theme: Wonder and Humility
What does this chapter show us about God's greatness?

Day 31 — Proverbs 31
Theme: Virtue and Strength
What qualities of wisdom and strength do we want to grow in?

READING CONTRACT

This agreement is made between (Keeper of the Flame) and (Emerging Leader) to establish a shared commitment to growing through reading.

Purpose:

Because reading builds knowledge, sharpens thinking, and equips us to lead well, (adult name) agrees to encourage and reward (emerging leader name) for their investment in reading.

Reward Options:

You may choose one or combine both.

Option A: Pay-Per-Page

- $0.10 per page read, including prefaces and tables of contents (as long as these are read).
- Minimum reward: $1.00 per book
- Suggested cap: $25.00 per book, based on page count or budget

Option B: Points-to-Rewards

- 1 point per page read
- Points may be exchanged for special rewards:

Points	Reward
500	Family outing or activity pass
750	$25 gift card
1,000	$50 toward a wish list item
2,000+	A weekend trip, experience, or special privilege

Customize the reward list together and post it somewhere visible.

Stewardship Plan:

To build wise money habits and a generous heart, the reward money (or value) will be split as follows:

- 10% Giving – Tithe or donate to a mission, church, or a cause of their choice
- 45% Saving – For education, future goals, or long-term dreams
- 45% Spending – For personal enjoyment with parental guidance

Book Report Requirements:

For each book completed, (emerging leader name) agrees to submit a one-page written report that includes:

1. Book Title
2. Author
3. A summary of the book's main idea or storyline
4. A description of the key lessons or takeaways
5. A brief reflection on how this book challenged or inspired them, and how they might apply what they learned in life, faith, or leadership

The report should demonstrate thoughtfulness, clarity, and personal engagement—not just a recap, but a reflection.

Duration:

This contract is valid for one year from the date below and may be renewed annually unless either party chooses to end or revise it.

Signed on this ___ day of ___________, 20___.

____

(Emerging Leader's Name & Signature)

____

(Keeper of the Flame's Name & Signature)

Because every great reader is a future leader... and every emerging leader is a keeper of the flame.

ABOUT THE AUTHOR

Dr. Tracey C. Jones is an author, publisher, podcaster, certified business coach, speaker, veteran, and international leadership expert—but at her core, she is a disciple committed to helping others live transformed lives. Raised by the legendary Charlie "Tremendous" Jones—a man who lived Romans 12:2—Tracey grew up immersed in Scripture, service, and shelves full of life-changing books. Her father often said, "*You'll be the same person five years from now as you are today except for two things: the people you meet and the books you read.*" Tracey took that message to heart and has spent her life helping others do the same.

A graduate of the U.S. Air Force Academy and decorated Gulf War and Bosnian War veteran, Tracey went on to serve in leadership roles in high tech, defense contracting, and publishing. She holds an MBA in Global Management and a Ph.D. in Leadership Studies from Lancaster Bible College.

Today, as President of Tremendous Leadership and T3 Solutions, Inc., Tracey carries forward the flame, equipping parents, mentors, and guardians to pass the torch of faith, wisdom, and leadership to the next generation. She is the author of 13 books, including a series of children's stories that use her rescue pets to teach timeless truths.

Tracey speaks worldwide—from prison book clubs to European classrooms to women's ministries in Africa. She lives in Pennsylvania with her tremendous husband, Mike, and their dogs, continuing to fan into flame the gifts of God in everyone she meets.

BOOKS BY DR. TRACEY C. JONES

True Blue Leadership: Top Ten Ways to Lead Your Pack
Saucy Aussie Living: The Top 10 Tricks for Getting a Second Leash on Life
Beyond Tremendous: Raising the Bar on Life
A Message to Millennials: What Your Parents Didn't Tell You and Your Employer Needs You to Know
SPARK: Five Essentials to Ignite the Greatness Within
Burnett or Bridgett: A Tale of Two Employees
The Art of Tremendous: Ten Tips for Life
SPARK: Keeper of the Flame for Emerging Leaders

Children's Books:

From Underdog to Wonderdog
Boxcar Indy: Square Dog in a Round World
Boxcar Indy Goes to Doggyworld
No, No, Roscoe!
Pawsitive Purrsonality Plus

To explore more books, courses, publishing, and leadership resources, visit www.TremendousLeadership.com.
For business coaching, speaking, training, or consulting, connect with Tracey directly at www.TraceyCJones.com.

Connect with Dr. Jones in LinkedIn
https://www.linkedin.com/in/drtraceycjones/

🎧 Listen to the Tremendous Leadership PodcastAvailable on YouTube, Apple Podcasts, Spotify, and wherever you listen to podcasts. https://tremendousleadership.com/pages/podcast